I have had the pleasure . . . and a great pleasure it was . . . to have read Gianni's book, and I strongly recommend it to everyone in the investment/trading "business." Eyes will be opened to what is actually going on in the broader world, but most especially to what is going on in China as that nation leaps from lifestyles of the eighteenth and nineteenth century directly into the twenty-second century, and, most importantly, they are not going back.

Gianni understands that, and through the metaphor of his Porsche-owning electrician, we are able to see more clearly what the future shall be in the world of commerce and commodities, and if Gianni's electrician plays his hand properly his next car won't be a Porsche, it will be a Bentley.

—*Dennis Gartman*
editor/publisher, The Gartman Letter

It's an engaging journey through the worlds of investing and emerging markets. Readable and thought-provoking, this book should be interesting and valuable to both rookie and veteran investors.

—*Ross Beaty*
founder, Pan American Silver Corp.

An eye opener! What will it take to build the green economy of the future? Gianni provides valuable insights.

—*Stuart McNish*
founder, Conversations That Matter

Finally, a readable, common-sense review of the implications of emerging markets. Long overdue!

—*Don Lindsay*
CEO, Teck Resources

MY ELECTRICIAN DRIVES A PORSCHE?

Investing in the Rise of the
New Spending Class

GIANNI KOVACEVIC

Published in the United States of America by Greenleaf Book Group Press
Austin, Texas
www.gbgpress.com

Published in Canada by Granville Island Publishing Ltd.
212 – 1656 Duranleau St.
Vancouver, BC, Canada V6H 3S4
www.granvilleislandpublishing.com

Published concurrently in Germany as *Mein Elektriker Fährt Einen Porsche?* by
FinanzBuch Verlag

Distributed by Greenleaf Book Group

For ordering information or special discounts for bulk purchases, please contact
Greenleaf Book Group at PO Box 91869, Austin, TX 78709, 512.891.6100.

Distributed in Canada by Granville Island Publishing
For ordering information or special discounts for bulk purchases in Canada,
please contact Granville Island Publishing at 604.688.0320, 1.877.688.0320 or
info@granvilleislandpublishing.com

Text design and composition by Omar Gallegos and Granville Island Publishing
Cover design by Greenleaf Book Group and Sheila Parr
Edited by Kyle Hawke and Greenleaf Book Group

Cataloging-in-Publication data is available.

USA and International Print ISBN: 978-1-62634-251-4

Canada Print ISBN: 978-1-92699-167-2

eBook ISBN: 978-1-62634-271-2

Part of the Tree Neutral® program, which offsets the number of
trees consumed in the production and printing of this book by
taking proactive steps, such as planting trees in direct proportion
to the number of trees used: www.treeneutral.com

TreeNeutral®

Printed in the United States of America on acid-free paper

15 16 17 18 19 20   10 9 8 7 6 5 4 3 2 1

First Edition

This book is dedicated to my heroes:

NJ for believing,
CG for always being there,
RB for taking that chance,
FH for wisdom,
and FCD for letting me in.

You can never comprehend
how much of a difference you have made.

Excerpt from the speech
"Citizenship in a Republic"

"It is not the critic who counts; not the man who points out how the strong man stumbles, or where the doer of deeds could have done them better.

"The credit belongs to the man who is actually in the arena, whose face is marred by dust and sweat and blood; who strives valiantly; who errs, who comes short again and again, because there is no effort without error and shortcoming; but who does actually strive to do the deeds; who knows great enthusiasms, the great devotions; who spends himself in a worthy cause; who at the best knows in the end the triumph of high achievement, and who at the worst, if he fails, at least fails while daring greatly, so that his place shall never be with those cold and timid souls who neither know victory nor defeat."

Delivered by Teddy Roosevelt
at the Sorbonne in Paris, France
April 23, 1910

Contents

Preface

I once was told that learning is as natural to a human being as blooming is to perennial flowers—it just happens. Much in the same way, adolescent curiosities shape our lifelong desires, and hopefully, bestow some level of wisdom. Socrates, once thought to be the wisest man in the universe, admitted, "I know one thing: that I know nothing." I then ask myself, how could I, a person surely eclipsed by countless scholars, possibly present a book about the ramifications of population growth?

In Steve Jobs' 2005 commencement address to Stanford's graduating class, he noted that life is a bunch of dots that eventually start connecting—a special thanks to Frank Giustra for pointing that out to me. The title of this book refers to an electrician who drives a Porsche, however, as one will read, the underlying thesis has nothing to do with fast cars. Moreover, the idea is for readers to gain a greater understanding of the demographic shift taking place around the world due to urbanization, and the role commodities play as the keystone underpinning any economy.

Serendipitously enough, my dots did connect, just as Messieurs Jobs and Giustra suggested they would. An electrician who is obsessed with technology in the 1990s and consumer growth in the 2000s unexpectedly becomes an expert in the core building block that makes them both possible: copper. So the story you are about to enjoy, told as a tale between two buddies, celebrates a role reversal as the life experiences of the younger electrician enable him to share his unique perspectives with his Baby Boomer doctor friend.

It should also be noted that I spent my entire childhood reading encyclopedias and *National Geographic* magazines. This foundation would spawn a passion, leading me to follow some of the great thinkers and economic historians of our time such as: Fareed Zakaria, Niall Ferguson, Frank Holmes, Don Coxe, and the green-metal maven himself, Robert Friedland. Their influence throughout this book is obvious.

Life will always kick sand in your eyes, so it becomes a never-ending task to surround oneself with heroes that act as protective goggles. I have been very fortunate to have incredible people around me to champion so many of my crazy ideas; thus I acknowledge and honor anyone who gave me a chance, anywhere along the way. This beautiful sentiment, from my fellow Pacific Northwesterner, sums up precisely how I will try, surely in vain, to somehow pay each one of them back.

Gianni Kovacevic

"If you are successful, it is because somewhere, sometime, someone gave you a life or an idea that started you in the right direction. Remember also that you are indebted to life until you help some less fortunate person, just as you were helped."

Melinda Gates

Foreword

Few people appreciate that their lives depend on copper and other natural resources. From the moment you wake up in your climate-controlled home to when you go to bed at night and set your alarm on your mobile phone, you are consuming natural resources that make life as you know it possible on Earth. The roof over your head, your car, your computer, your plumbing, your heating and cooling systems, your telecommunications—chances are they all contain copper. And as our global population surges past seven billion and millions of people in China and India continue the inevitable human pursuit of progress and migrate from farms to cities, demand for copper and other resources will only grow.

I've been talking to investors about these themes of emerging markets' growth and urbanization for many years. Now, Gianni Kovacevic's artful storytelling takes curious investors on an exciting journey around the world to explore and discover these trends and their unexpected impact on the resource market. *My Electrician Drives a Porsche?* is an interesting allegory of human progress and opportunity.

Frank E. Holmes

1

The office call

It was Wednesday, and Wednesday is my favorite day of the week. First and foremost because, for some strange reason, it's always easier to find a good parking spot on a Wednesday—a small luxury that has been in short supply in Seattle ever since I bought the Lincoln SUV I'd been driving to work.

The average life expectancy for a female living in the United States is 82.2 years, just a little over a nice round 80. But if you happen to be a male, like myself, you have just a measly 77.4 years to look forward to. Luckily, my level of income somewhat negates the limitations of my chromosomes and bumps me back up another two or three years, depending on whose research you're reading.

The point being that I don't have time to spend ten minutes every day looking for a parking space. I'd actually taken the time and done the measurements—the Lincoln is about six inches too wide to fit into most available spaces. It felt like a good fit for my daily commute when I bought it, but skip forward to today and I'd have to admit that it seems a tad absurd. What once felt roomy now felt bloated. That isn't to suggest that it's a bad vehicle. It's great, really. It's got a handsome design and a lavish interior, rides smoothly, handles well, and stops on a relatively small dime. Even so, since my wife and I divorced and I'd moved into a fixer-upper less than ten minutes away from work, door-to-door, the Lincoln simply no longer made sense. Also, if I'm going to be perfectly blunt, it made me feel old. It's a vehicle that a married man of my age and stature is expected to drive, but now that I was single for the first time since my teens, it represented everything about my life with which I no longer identified. It was predictable and safe and I wanted something a little more "present," if you will. In that vein, I was gradually working my way up to cycling to work but hadn't quite made it past the part where I actually got on my bike and did it.

I digress. The second reason I love Wednesdays is because they make me thankful I chose to become a family doctor. While medicine is an inexact science, medical practice is still, in my opinion, an art form, one that I've mastered in my own way. On no other day was this more evident than Wednesdays, where nearly all my duties as a physician boiled down to simply listening to my patients.

Wednesdays are predictable and serene, qualities in a day I have truly come to admire. Serene, because it's when my practice seems to hit its natural weekly lull in terms of foot traffic. The regulars schedule their check-ups at the beginning of the week, while those with some nagging, neglected, or nonexistent issue prefer to wait until Thursday or Friday to come in.

Ah yes, Wednesdays: uneventful and boring, yet perfect—my own private infinity pool of crosswords, jazz radio,
and those obnoxious business TV shows that I love to hate.
At this point in my career it doesn't even bother me too much
when a patient cancels since it gives me the freedom to kick
back, watch my stocks, and maybe even read a newspaper
if I get really lucky. It's bizarre really, how doing nothing in
my office now feels perfectly fine while, when I'm at home,
I feel the need to work constantly on something. It's as if my
work has become a hobby and my new home my actual job.

This time last year it would have been the opposite. I
was still a relentless busybody in the office, while an absolute
loafer at home. Even though I'd spend lots of my time
watching do-it-yourself shows, I never actually got around to
doing any, well, do-it-yourselfing.

The diagnosis for such a *volte-face* of behavior is quite
obvious. I attribute it to the two decades I spent obsessively
flipping between PGA golf and home improvement shows.
It was an addiction that started off innocently enough with
This Old House on PBS and quickly escalated with the advent
of reality TV. After the dust settled on my divorce, I made
a rather bold move and purchased a three-bedroom, 2,500
square-foot, window-happy split-level built in the style
of early West Coast modern architecture. It definitely had
potential, but all that potential rested on me getting off the
couch and doing the work. It was a grand, exciting project—
the only problem was that I had to live in it in the meantime.
Bob Vila would have loved it if he ever had the guts to brave
the Pacific Northwest's endemic rains. Today was such a day,
the dictionary definition of coffee-loving, umbrella-toting
Seattle.

So now I find time to relax in between patients and spend
my nights doing my best impersonation of a handyman,
putting all that wasted time behind the boob tube to use as I

renovate my new house, room by room. Mostly though, I'm still just making a mess of things.

As for additional methods of relaxation, I enjoy casually obsessing over my financial situation. The recession was not kind to my generation. Although relatively insulated from the dire straits that hit more than a few of my cohorts, I was still wary of risk and exposure. I had friends with exceptional professional careers who lost half their wealth in the crash and were now postponing their retirement until sixty-five, some even going so far as to say they'd be working until seventy. Good grief. I had similar concerns, but I took a more proactive and defensive posture toward my portfolio and assets.

That said, I knew as soon as I walked up to the front door, shaking my soaked umbrella, that this particular Wednesday wasn't going to be as tranquil as I expected. What tipped me off was the giant floating birthday balloon I could see waiting for me in the lobby, accompanied by my receptionist, the ever-lovely Pamela, smiling from ear to ear.

"Good morning. And happy birthday, Doctor Anderson!" she cried, all a-tingle as I walked in. I guess I'd gotten so caught up in overthinking my renovation and finding the perfect parking spot that I completely forgot it was my own birthday.

"Ah, yes. Thank you very much, Pamela," I muttered, thinking that maybe I *did* know it was my birthday but didn't want to acknowledge it. They all sort of blend together after you hit fifty anyways, so who's counting?

"Fifty-eight years young! And for that, I got you an açai berry protein power smoothie. It'll boost your energy and it's low on carbs so it's super healthy and I won't take no for an answer so you might as well have it now."

Pamela always talked excitedly. She never seemed to take breaths.

"Oh, great. Thanks for this. I'll just go and get a coffee first if you don't mind."

"Doctor Anderson, you *are* a doctor, remember?"

"Oh, yes, that's true. And as a doctor, I'm very aware of the repercussions of caffeine withdrawal. So, in this practice's best interest, it's always coffee first, health second."

"Sheesh."

At least the day's schedule was predictable. The lovely Mrs. Chau, whose osteoarthritis was acting up again, was coming in at ten. Good ol' Cal Vernon after that, which if I were to proffer a guess, was coming in due to a case of indigestion he'd once again mistaken for a heart attack.

After serving your community as a family doctor for almost thirty years, you learn to anticipate your patients' ailments and recognize patterns so you can predict what they are coming in for. There are the regulars, like Chau and Vernon, who essentially need an empathetic ear and a dose of reassurance, and then there are those who drift in every few years for sporadic and usually important reasons, either due to an emergency or from some exotic tropical bug. As I looked through the rest of my daysheet, I noticed a name I didn't immediately recognize—Johnny Rossi.

Johnny Rossi . . . who is that? That name rings a bell.

"Who's this Rossi fellow?" I asked.

"Hmm. Let me check. He hasn't come in for a few years, actually. His profession is listed as . . ." She leafed through his file. ". . . electrician."

"Oh, yes. How can I have possibly forgotten? Younger guy. I met him quite a while ago when he was doing some electrical work for us at the old house. Great kid. Loved to travel in his spare time, if I recall."

The day went along like any other. Mrs. Chau complained about the inflammation on her leg, but mostly wanted to talk about her granddaughter's stellar grades, which she attributed to genetics. Cal did indeed have some acute gastrointestinal issues, but mostly wanted to gripe about the current condition of the Mariners, especially our bullpen. I didn't mind having an extended chat as baseball, along with investing, was something I always had extra time for.

During my break, I noticed my largest current holding flash across the screen, a good sign. After watching for a few more minutes, it seemed that my portfolio was as resilient as ever, especially Coca-Cola, which was riding on a multi-year high. Coca-Cola doesn't get a lot of hype compared to companies like Apple or whatever flavor of the week is dominating the tech market, but for me it was exactly what I wanted: solid, dependable, predictable, and profitable. Aside from my Coca-Cola stock, corporate bonds had been the investment with which I'd been most satisfied and which suited my lifestyle best. If I needed to make a withdrawal in order to pay for something involved with my renovations, it was a relatively painless process. Otherwise, I knew my bonds would be sitting there, preserving my capital while providing me with some extra quarterly income. I could feel my blood pressure drop and my heart rate ease into a flawless seventy beats per minute just thinking about them.

I noticed it was getting close to quitting time just as Johnny arrived for the last appointment of the day. When Pamela ushered him into my office, it was clear that he had done quite a bit of growing up since I had last seen him. Even so, he still had a youthful glow for a man in his midthirties.

"Hello, Johnny. It's been awhile."

"Yes, it has. Time flies."

"How have you been?"

"I've been excellent. Nice birthday balloons, Doc!"

"Oh, yes. *Those.*"

"How have you been?"

"Oh, you know. Coming to grips with my graying hair and other such thrills. You haven't been here for a while. When was your last check-up?" I asked.

"To be honest, you would know better than me."

"According to your file, it was over ten years ago, Johnny. Tsk tsk. While I appreciate that you haven't been seeing any other GPs behind my back, I'm still obligated to chastise you for not coming more often. Say, at least once a year."

"I know, I know. I'll prioritize it eventually."

"So where have you been?"

"Just really busy with work. And I've been doing a lot of traveling over the past few years as well."

"Just like my kids. Your generation certainly likes to enjoy itself. And I'll tell you what I've told them—it's all fun and games until you've got a mortgage to pay."

"To be honest, I'm more worried about this ankle that's been acting up than I am about making mortgage payments, Doc."

"Yes, well that's typical, isn't it? What's bothering you?"

"I twisted it a few months back on a hiking trip in the Swiss Alps and it still hasn't fully healed."

"Well, Johnny, I hate to break it to you, but you're not a teenager any more. If you're walking on it, you should be fine, but we'll check it out anyway."

"Sounds good."

"So, the Swiss Alps? Sounds expensive. How was it?"

"Fantastic. I go to Europe often—you know me and my languages. If you don't use 'em, you lose 'em."

"That's right. You're the guy who spoke, like, four or five languages, right? Can you move your ankle this way?"

"Guilty as charged, Doc," Johnny replied, slowly rotating his leg. "Being able to talk to the locals when you travel adds a lot of spice to any trip. But when I'm in China, my guidebook Mandarin isn't getting me too far."

"China? My God, you've traveled farther since your last check-up than I've managed in my entire life. Now, how is that fair? And how do you manage to get so much vacation time?"

"I just make it happen. Get busy living or get busy dying, Doc, that's my motto."

"Great motto. Do you mind if I borrow it?"

"Fill your boots."

"I just hope you're not as bad as my daughter when it comes to savings."

"That's her, right? Jenna?" he asked, pointing to a picture on my wall. "I haven't seen her since I worked on your place—guess that was ten years back."

"Yes, that's her."

"Is that the Grand Canyon?"

"Good eye," I nodded. "Yes, I took the kids there last summer."

"Hey, how is she? And Brady, was it?"

"Good memory," I offered. "I guess you met him back then, too."

"He'd already moved out by then, if my memory is good. How are they?"

"They're both fine, or so they say. They're taking me out to dinner tonight, and I'm sure I'll hear that money's tight for both of them," I sighed. "Brady's running a restaurant and Jenna's been teaching. She's only a bit younger than you and still hasn't paid off her student loans. I worry about her. Both of them, actually."

"That's rough, Doc."

"If I give you one tip, Johnny, it's that the power of compound interest is truly the eighth wonder of the world. With all these trips, are you able to have any savings? It sounds like you've got a very flexible job, but you're never too young to begin appreciating the true power of the buck and the discipline of steady, predictable contributions to retirement and general investing. Trust me, I've been doing it for over thirty years now."

"Whoa there, Doc! Easy on the lectures. Of course I have some savings. Give me some credit. As they say: no money, no honey!"

"All right, I apologize. You've clearly got a good head on your shoulders, but I just can't help but wonder when I hear about young people who travel as much as you do. Perhaps I'm jealous. You make me think of what I'd be like if I hadn't gone to med school, if I'd had more fun instead. I've done all right, though. I was able to buy my first home in my twenties because I was disciplined and followed a few basic rules that ended up paying dividends."

"Thanks for the concern, Doc. Honestly though, I'm fine. I know you probably think all us Gen Xers are hard up just because you Boomers didn't exactly give us too many options, but I'm doing pretty good."

"Oh, here we go with that old sob story. You sound just like Jenna."

"Hey, I sound a lot like anybody who came of age in the nineties when all the cheap real estate and cushy government jobs ran out. I'm not one to tar and feather an individual just because he happens to be a Boomer, but you must admit, you guys had it pretty easy."

"I know. The kids say the same thing. They feel it's going to be almost impossible to buy the kind of house that they grew up in. I'm sure it's the same with most of your friends."

"Yeah. I got a lot of friends that complain about getting the short end of the stick, but you must always look at the silver lining. Technology, for example. How well do you understand it?"

"Computers and whatnot?"

"I'm talking about all of it."

"Well, to be blunt, not much. I bought an iPad but haven't quite figured out how to download, upload, or reload a damn thing on it. That's your generation's department!"

"I feel the same way. It *is* my generation's department, and I see that as a huge opportunity. And it has been just that. Unlike other Gen Xers, I often feel like I'm the luckiest guy in the world."

"Come again?"

"What I mean is that being in the right place at the right time can be the luckiest thing that can happen to someone. You just need to notice opportunity when it comes knocking."

"Well, I'm glad to see you're so optimistic. In fact, if you're also feeling industrious, I was thinking of something before you came. You see, I'm working on a new house and . . ."

"You moved?"

"Yes, but well, that's a long story. And long story short, I've got a new place and I could really use your help. I've been trying to hook up some fancy automation system that will control my lights, air-conditioning, and other things. When they sold me this equipment, they warned me it would be a little more advanced than the average weekend warrior could tackle. I have to admit it's more complicated than watching home improvement shows for twenty years. So how about this—you come by and help me out? I promise I just need some supervised guidance, then we can have a couple beers and I'll let you in on a few of my investment and forced savings secrets."

"Your secrets?"

"Hey, I've got a couple aces up my sleeve when it comes to investing. What do you say? Is it a deal?"

"Okay, sure. I'll bite. When?"

"How's this Saturday? 10 a.m.?"

"Sounds good."

"I guess I should ask. How much do you typically charge?"

"There's a great joke I like to use, and it's a perfect way to answer your question."

"Shoot. I love a good joke."

"A plumber fixes a leaky sink for a doctor and hands him a bill for a thousand dollars. The doctor yells, 'This is outrageous! Even I don't charge that much!' The plumber replies, 'Neither did I when I was a doctor!'"

"Har-de-har-har. Don't get cute, Johnny. Two can play that game," I laughed. "I'll make it worth your while. Plus, you never know, you may even benefit from some of the stock ideas I have."

"Sounds good, Doc. And for the record, my house call is on the house, but that's only for the first two hours of consultation."

"Deal," I said as I stretched out my hand.

"Deal."

"Oh, and Johnny, make sure to elevate that ankle whenever it's feeling sore. Maybe use an ice pack if it helps. Eventually, it'll be good as new. These things take a few months. Just stay away from anything jarring."

"Thanks, Doc."

There is something satisfying when one generation can help another. We Baby Boomers, born during the surge of global births after World War II, knew the value of hard work. The so-called lost generation like Johnny and my kids, dubbed "Generation X," those who entered the work force in the nineties, blamed us older folks for their lack of opportunities.

Over the past thirty years, I met most of my kids' friends, who ranged from grunge-style rockers to university whiz-kids. Were their collective complaints about Boomers justified? Perhaps. However, they certainly had the advantage of being born at the right time to take full advantage of the technological revolution. There were not many twenty-something billionaires in my time like there are today. Clearly, there are pros and cons between our generations, but it gave me a fuzzy warm feeling inside to be able to help Johnny with some investment advice in turn for his help with my renovations.

Wires and hamburgers
as the modern portfolio

Saturdays were the absolute inverse of Wednesdays. Rather than sitting at the office watching Bloomberg or having lengthy conversations about the weather with octogenarians, I was a man of action. I had no regrets about becoming a doctor—how could anyone? Still, truth be told, I always wanted to be an architect, even from a young age.

Even though I was only renovating a house, it felt as if I was finally able to live out that dream. My favorite architect was Frank Lloyd Wright, which is the main reason I purchased this particular house, the closest thing available to a Wright original that I could afford. One of his quotes that I read in my twenties had stuck with me until this day:

We are no longer truly simple. We no longer live in simple terms or places. Life is a more complex struggle now. It is now valiant to be simple, a courageous thing to even want to be simple. It is a spiritual thing to comprehend what simplicity means.

The older I became, the more the quote rang true. More than anything, I think undertaking this grand venture was an attempt to simplify my life and forget the complexities of the world that had dogged me over the last decade. The irony was that, in reality, it was a ridiculously complicated project.

By the time the doorbell rang, I had lost myself in a box of electrical cables, completely forgetting that I had invited Johnny over to help me figure out all the wiring required to get this so-called automation system online. The very thought of figuring out where to hide the countless cables required forced me to release an audible sigh. While I definitely needed Johnny's know-how, I was also hoping he'd help out with the electrical system in general. And to be brutally honest with myself, it was going to be nice having someone around to help me climb the ever-escalating reno-mountain I had nicknamed "El Grande."

I'd barely had a soul over since moving in, and the place was a mess of supplies, tools, and empty pizza boxes. I was definitely not projecting the image of a responsible family doctor, but the freedom to live like I was back in my college dorm days was, in its own way, liberating. I made a hurried attempt to tidy up on my way to the door, but before I got there, Johnny had already let himself in and was keenly surveying the damage.

"Hey there, Johnny. Thanks for coming by. I'd nearly forgotten and was about to run out and get some supplies. I've really bitten off more than I can chew with these renovations, which I've dubbed 'El Grande.'"

"The Big One. Great nickname, Doc."

"I'm trying to boost my weekend-warrior ego by pretending I'm a hands-on guy, but I'm going to need to call in favors from unsuspecting patients or friends to get me over the finish line."

"Not a problem. I'm just doing some running around today, anyway."

"So it's another day off for you, I suppose?"

"Come on, Doc. Weekends are for reading, fraternizing, and fitness. And not in that order," Johnny joked.

"For a globe-trotting spendthrift, you lead a rather structured life, Johnny. You're going to have to enlighten me about your Zen practice. Any stories you have will add some interest to my life cooped up in here all day. Come on in and don't worry about your shoes. It's a mess anyway."

We walked through the foyer and into the living room, which after all these months was still full of unpacked boxes. It's funny how quickly my attention to tidiness dissipated after the divorce. Cathleen had been a lovely wife. I can't really fault her in any way, but she was definitely far more preoccupied with keeping the house in order than I ever was. She broke stuff and I fixed it; I made a mess of things and she set them straight—it was our thing.

"Please excuse the state of this place. As you can probably see, I'm still getting things in order. By the way, I was half-laughing about your plumber joke the other day. I honestly have no idea how much tradesmen make these days."

"That depends, Doc, there are electricians and then . . . there are *electricians*."

"I'm starting to get the feeling that you're the second kind; the kind that has found some special niche and charges twice as much as the typical, run-of-the-mill wire-puller."

"Relax. I'm not here to charge you at all. I'm here because I enjoy your company. And you clearly don't remember, but when I worked on your other house, I stayed super late during a heat wave to get your air-conditioning up and running. As an added thanks, you gave me your old set of TaylorMade golf clubs, remember?"

"Oh, yeah. You old son-of-a-gun," I smiled. "That's right. We stayed until ten at night, and you kept complimenting me on that old set. Well, I hope they improved your game. I know my new clubs did nothing for mine."

"I'm a ten handicap now, and I still use them to this day. Thanks again."

"Well then, I guess I can go ahead and take some liberties with you, but just for today. Basically, I bought this new home automation system and want to wire it up so I can get all its features. But I can't seem to get everything figured out, and there are a lot of variables and different types of cable for the Internet, stereo, TV, and speakers. They told me it wasn't easy but they forgot to tell me you need a PhD in electrical engineering to figure it all out."

"Wow! Look at that pile of cables! You know you're supposed to keep them in their boxes until you install them, Doc."

Johnny fiddled with the instruction manual a bit, then walked around and checked out all the pieces of equipment, one by one. As he fumbled around the various components of modern technology, I thought to myself about how quickly they would become obsolete.

"First of all, this is going to take more than just a few hours on a Saturday," he said.

"I was worried you'd say that."

"Secondly, there's a better way than hardwiring all this outdated stuff."

"What do you mean?"

"You should probably just go for a wireless system. It would cut down on the clutter and most of this stuff will work just perfectly. I hate to say it, but I think that guy at the home improvement shop sold you a bill of goods."

"You'll have to forgive me, Johnny. I haven't updated anything in years. What exactly is a wireless system?"

"It's what it sounds like, Doc, a system without wires. Works like Wi-Fi."

"Yes, all right, Wi-Fi. I do know what that is. Jenna set it up for us in the old place a few years back and the guy installed it here when he put in the Internet and cable. Cathleen told me to make sure he did. So are you suggesting I just scrap this altogether and pick up a new one?"

"I'm just saying that there are much better options available. Technology is moving faster than you may think. I can let you know what system I have. It's super simple and works great—unless you'll be hosting any rock concerts here. Then you'll want something snazzier."

"Nope. No huge parties, but you've probably got some newfangled fancy system. I may be a doctor, but I'm not trying to spend an arm and a leg."

"Not at all an issue. The price of electronics, as we all know, continues to go down. Let me guess, you bought this system on the discount floor, right?"

"Well, yes. They told me it was just as good as the new stuff, only way cheaper as it was an older model."

"If you pay peanuts, you get monkeys."

"I know, I know. At least we're getting somewhere. Boy, where were you last week when I needed a consultant?"

"You could get something just as good but way more convenient. For now, we'll take the savings you realized on this unit and just get it done. How *is* Cathleen, by the way?"

"Oh, she's good. Her practice is going strong, I understand." I sighed, knowing where the conversation went from here. "Earlier this year, we were divorced, thus the mess."

"I'm sorry to hear that. Is everything okay?"

"Everything's fine. We're still friends. It just wasn't working any more as a marriage. I won't bore you with the details because it's the same story with so many couples living in an empty nest. I guess we were just both looking to start a new chapter. We ultimately decided that she should get the old house as her work was so close by and I was commuting forty-five minutes each way. So here I am, living in El Grande."

"Well, then here's to the next chapter. Onward and upward!"

As Johnny hoisted an imaginary "cheers," I realized that this was the first real instance of socializing I'd had at the new place since I moved in. It was great to chat with someone who was in no way connected to my marriage or practice.

"This seems like quite the project you've got going on here. What's your plan?"

"Basically, I've always been in love with West Coast modern architecture. I'm somewhat of an aficionado. But with Cathleen and the kids, it just wasn't feasible to find a home in that style that met all of our needs. So in a way, I'm living out a dream."

"Great. But this looks like a lot of work."

"I can do most of it, or that's my plan anyways, and I'm trying not to get any contractors involved. Stuff like the bathroom and kitchen or walls and flooring is definitely realistic, but as you can see I'm hopeless when it comes to the more technical aspects, such as electricity and plumbing. But enough about me. How has the last decade treated you? Are you married? Still with that same company?"

"Not married yet. I've been busy traveling and trying to figure out how everything in our world works."

"Sheesh. I cringe when I think about how much of that gallivanting money you could have invested. Back at the old house, we talked about some stocks you were dabbling in. I hope you at least stuck with that."

"Things have been, how shall I say, educational," Johnny said, with a mischievous glimmer in his eyes. "The ups and downs since the 2008 financial crisis haven't been easy but there certainly have been a fair share of opportunities."

"Opportunities? What have you been drinking? Or smoking? I can't comment on your portfolio but I've been investing longer than you've been alive, Johnny. I would say that average investors have had their portfolios turned upside down, period, and now it's tougher than ever to make consistent gains."

"Where do you get your investment advice from, Doc?"

"I've read the *Wall Street Journal* almost every day for thirty years. Now, with these financial shows on twenty-four hours a day, I have it on as background noise seven days a week. But we're bombarded by so-called news from all directions and information moves so quickly now, even if you're on top of it as I consider myself to be, the computer traders are one or five steps ahead of guys like you and me."

"Why even bother then? If you don't think you can keep up, why not just stick to safe and steady, like exchange-traded funds, blue-chip stocks, or mutual funds?"

"I do, and that's *all* I do. Remember the dot-com bomb? How much money was lost due to such overwhelming stupidity? Were the tech analysts who crowded Wall Street, and the investors that followed them, really going to justify the insane valuations of companies like www.sell-me-something-stupid-online.com or www.this-is-really-high-tech-so-it-just-has-to-work.com? Really, what the hell was everyone thinking?"

"I know. Most investments in these 'virtual' companies went to money heaven," Johnny agreed. "Who didn't lose their shirt getting sucked into the vortex? It's funny how every bubble ends the same, and then everyone becomes an armchair general after the war. However, the best-in-class ideas with strong management worked out and ended up turning huge profits for patient and, more importantly, educated investors."

"Sure, Johnny. And I'm supposed to know which one in twenty would work? I was educated like every other sucker out there."

"Were you?"

"I was reading the same thing everyone else was. Probably even more so."

"So what was your big takeaway from all that heartache? You followed the herd and were dealt the same fate, so you deserved it?"

"After the dot-com bust, I began investing in those ETFs and mutual funds. Not just any mutual funds—I'm talking about the best of the best, fully secured real estate funds and blue-chip products. And then what? We got hit by falsified real estate ownership, supported by the hyenas on Wall Street, that caused the largest default in credit in living memory. That loss of faith in the overall system cascaded into the 2008 financial crisis and *poof!* fifty percent of the average investor's value vaporized. Everyone I knew was directly exposed and the core of everything, real estate, was 'securitized.'"

"Tell me about it. We all lived it. But never forget that in every crisis, there is an opportunity."

"While that crisis bred more bubble and confidence destroyers, the euro crisis, and the municipal bond implosion? Who could see that coming? Entire countries going bankrupt! Cities and counties right here in the United States. Another *poof!* like a fart in the wind—all that value and worse, so much investor confidence, was gone. Nothing worked. Even that crisis-grade staple, gold, fell after a brief initial surge."

"Wow, Doc. You're a real live doomsayer. So what are you telling me? Don't invest anymore?"

"Of course you have to invest. Personally, I just stay away from anything I don't understand, and I stick to the things I know and trust. Businesses that have been around for decades that sell products we cannot live without are the most likely to be here for decades to come. I buy and hold Coca-Cola and McDonald's, I'll buy Microsoft, and I'll hold the steady and stable dividends that they pay, and I'm very confident that they are not going to go bankrupt like the country of Greece or the city of Detroit."

"Seems logical enough. What kind of returns can you expect with these kinds of investments?"

"I'm pulling a steady seven or eight percent, sometimes even as high as ten. Best of all, I don't lose any sleep and I'm fully liquid. I aggregate my retirement plan and my savings plan into one diversified account. I figure, why should I pay some mutual-fund manager to buy blue chips when I can do it myself and save the fees they charge?"

"So what you're trying to tell me is that I should strive for a balanced portfolio of diversified, dividend-paying stocks and just sit back and enjoy the ride."

"Remember, Johnny, the eighth wonder of the world is compound interest. There is a simple rule that you can plug into any compounded rate of interest and that is seventy-two, the 'rule of 72.'"

"I've read this in books before: when you divide your compounded rate into seventy-two, it tells you the amount of years it takes for your capital to double. If you're getting a ten-percent compounded annual rate of return then, divided by seventy-two, your capital doubles every 7.2 years?"

"Yes indeed, Johnny. That is the key to investing—patience, steady contributions, and no overnight get-rich-quick schemes. They just don't work and you'll end up losing most of your money, not multiplying it."

Johnny looked around and, among all the rubbish, noticed a Big Mac container, grabbed it, and passed it over to me.

"Doc, have you ever wondered how much a Big Mac really costs?" he asked, thoughtfully.

"Ha! Well, I guess I should know since I just ate one. I'm going to guess around $4.50."

"What about twenty-five years ago?"

Now, he was challenging me, though I couldn't guess why.

"No idea. I'd have to think about it. Two dollars? Three dollars? Isn't there some website where you can find that kind of stuff?"

"Absolutely."

Johnny whipped out his smartphone, flicked his fingers across the screen for a few seconds, and showed me. Twenty-five years ago, the price of a Big Mac was $2.20, and in 1980, it was a dollar.

"Do you know what the original price for a Big Mac was when it was introduced in 1968?"

"I guess I should, as those were my teenage years and I was eating them by the bagful, but I have no idea."

"Forty-nine cents."

"Okay, and . . . ?"

"Do you know how much oil is needed to make one Big Mac?"

"Hah! I know how much is in one—too much—and it's probably killing me. As a doctor, I should know better, but I'm a bachelor now, so I think I'm allowed to have the occasional dietary lapse. Hey, speaking of Big Macs, McDonald's has been a great long-term company. If I had only just invested in McDonald's in ninety-eight—before the dot-com bomb, before the real estate collapse, before the 2008 financial crisis, and before the euro and civil bond collapse—where would I be? In fact, that's a great question that will help illustrate the power of patient value investing."

"That's not the kind of oil I'm talking about, Doc. What I'm trying to get at is what it actually takes to make a Big Mac—or anything for that matter, but we'll just stick to the Big Mac for this example. You have the cattle for the beef, wheat for the bread, oil—not cooking oil, but the black stuff from the ground to deliver the products and enable the processing—and then there's accounting, overhead, and so much more. Oil is a commodity, and we need all the commodities to make Coca-Cola possible, or the underlying building blocks of Microsoft, Google, all your home-improvement stuff, and everything else around us. How did the core elements of the economy fare the past ten or twenty years? Have you been following that?"

"Wait a minute, if you're talking about commodities . . . That's trading! Have you not heard one word I just said?"

"I'm not talking about trading commodities, Doc, I'm talking about inflation. If the cost of a Big Mac, and everything around us, increases exponentially with inflation then what is your real rate of return on your seven-to-ten percent portfolio? Have you ever thought about that?"

Just then something sounding like a UFO signal came from Johnny's phone. The flying saucer repairman quickly checked it then clicked it off.

"Damn, I must run. How about we chat more about McDonald's and Big Macs next Saturday?"

"So that means you're going to help me work on El Grande?"

"Yeah, let's see how things go. For now, I don't have any trips planned and I find it fascinating to see how a well-educated Baby Boomer like yourself thinks, invests, and, yes, even renovates."

Johnny, who arrived with no tools and was dressed in what I could only imagine to be painfully overpriced designer jeans, found his way to the door. After a couple of minutes I realized that we didn't get much actual work done, but he had saved me dozens of hours and countless dollars by offering the most up-to-date and technically advanced advice that I needed. Staring at the empty Big Mac container, pictures of commodities rolled through my head like a ticker tape and I felt like a complete fool when I realized I hadn't a clue how much any real commodities cost, from beef to wheat to the metals in all the supplies lying around me. And his parting shot, inflation. Had I forgotten about inflation?

As I rushed outside to the driveway to see if I could intercept Johnny and ask him one more question, all I saw were the taillights of a bright red sports car racing away.

"Wow, nice car. Who's that?" my neighbor called over, jaw hanging from his chin.

"Um . . . my electrician."

"Your electrician drives a Porsche?"

"What?" I repeated, utterly bewildered. "My electrician drives a Porsche?"

Financial soap operas

Throughout the week I was reminded repeatedly of Johnny's Big Mac comment by a series of commercials that flashed through my financial shows. He'd made the point of asking me the difference in price between a Big Mac today and a Big Mac in the past. The more vexing part of the question was the second part, relating the price of ingredients to inflation. I was never the one who bought the groceries nor have I ever given any thought to the cost of what he called "the core elements of the economy." The relationship between these things and our stock talk was clearly more than just a few trivial facts that were going to help me when I watched *Jeopardy*. It seemed obvious that the price of a Big Mac goes up at about the same rate as inflation. Easy answer. Done. And yet, I had the sneaking suspicion that there must have been some greater meaning to the relevance of inflation with respect to one's investment portfolio.

Hamburgers and commodities were not the only thing that went over my head. One can only marvel at how an electrician can afford to drive around town in such a conspicuously expensive car. Something didn't sit right with me. Had I missed some vast redistribution of wealth while I was dutifully tending to my patients all these years? Or did I not hear the part where Johnny told me that he now owns a big firm with lots of employees and lucrative contracts? Maybe he came from a wealthy family, or perhaps I completely misinterpreted the situation and he's simply blowing all his profits on a car he can barely afford and now wants to start saving his hard-earned money? I thought about my Brady and Jenna, bless their live-in-the-moment hearts, and the staggering amounts of credit-card debt they'd racked up as consumers in our modern world.

By the time Saturday morning rolled around, I was half excited and half uneasy and I made sure I was outside in time for Johnny to pull up in his work van, half-hoping it would turn out to be a classic and perhaps even a bit beaten-up.

Boy, was I off. When he arrived, he cruised up to the curb in what appeared to be a brand-new, top-of-the-line Turbo model—I was no expert so couldn't be sure. Still, I instantly felt pangs of envy, and perhaps a little bit of regret, as I glanced over at my portly Lincoln.

"Ciao, Doc. You have a productive week?"

"Good morning, Johnny. Do you need a hand grabbing the tools out of your work van over there?"

"Funny, Doc. I'm guessing you've got a full set. You've seen every do-it-yourself show produced since the nineties, so you surely got the tools to match, no? Those fads usually go lockstep with the hand-to-wallet reflex."

"Okay, you got me there. I have a pretty damn good set. What I was alluding to was the fact that your work van . . . is a *Porsche!*"

"Just a little way to spoil myself for a job well done."

"You had a good year electrifying things?"

"You could put it that way. Or you could say it's nice when a plan comes together."

"You have my attention. And not to be snoopy, but just how good is the electrical trade these days? It looks like your plumber joke is about to become a shocking reality."

"Truth be told, I never intended to charge you a penny! Like I said last week, I'm genuinely interested in understanding how a middle-aged, well-educated Baby Boomer appreciates our changing world. Why don't we just say you're returning the favor by expanding my horizons with your perspective?"

"Well, if we're on the favor system, why don't you tell me what you're really up to these days. Besides traversing the globe, driving fast cars, and diagnosing the impact Big Macs have on society. My curiosity is piqued."

"Let's go inside and I'll tell you."

Johnny made his way to and through the garage door, so I shrugged and followed. Rather than reach for the tools, or even get direction about our task for the day, Johnny sat himself in the recliner and gave me a bizarre answer.

"I follow soap operas for a living," he grinned.

"Come again?" I replied, seating myself on my very dusty sofa.

"I follow social and financial soap operas, day in, day out. It's pretty hard to do that if you're punching the clock nine–to-five."

"So you're not an electrician anymore? Now I'm thoroughly confused. Why didn't you just tell me that in the first place? So you changed careers and now you're involved in the soap opera industry?"

"Not even close, Doc. You're overthinking things. I stopped working as a day-to-day electrician about ten years ago, and that's when I started taking my investments more seriously. I use the word soap opera as a descriptive way to demonstrate my level of commitment to how I follow my finances and our ever-changing world. For me, upping my game meant doing a little more than just reading the *Wall Street Journal* or buying into companies with 'green' in the name."

"So investing has become like a daily obsession for you. Is that what you mean when you use the term 'soap opera'?"

"That's it! Following financial markets as a daily affair has become one of the cornerstones of my ethical investment philosophy."

"So you're an investor now, not an electrician? The only people I've heard that stay at home all day trading stocks are those daredevil day-traders."

"Not me, that's not what I'm doing. I'm just an investor like you, but maybe my approach is a bit different. You see, folks like you might call me a 'speculator,' or even a 'high-risk investor,'" he smiled. "But am I?"

"Sure sounds like it. What in the hell are you investing in, anyways?"

"No offense, but most investors, and I do mean almost all of them, including you, take all their investable income— retirement savings, general savings, etcetera—and place it in mutual funds or blue-chip stocks, chasing dividends, and hopefully, some capital appreciation. Which are totally logical as core holdings for any portfolio, especially as you approach retirement."

"Which I hope will come well before my sixty-fifth birthday."

As I said that, I felt like I should be checking the clock.

"What many investors totally forget is how real inflation affects their overall returns. Have you given any thought to how your *real* spending power has been impacted in the past decade?"

"This comes back to your Big Mac question, doesn't it? And how a Big Mac and its components contribute to its price increase."

"Let's address that. There are many factors that push commodity prices higher and lower. What I meant by that question was, if most things consumers buy—the Big Mac being a well-known example—go up in price by five or six or seven percent annually, and investors are hoping to make seven to ten percent, what has happened to their real rate of return?"

"Basic arithmetic says it negates most of the return."

"Exactly. So, due to that fact, what has happened to your real spending power on a global basis?"

"My practical side is telling me I have more and more capital when I make my returns, but when you spoon-feed me in this way, my common sense is telling me my *real* spending power is being lost."

"There's a great term now being used to describe this phenomenon called 'reward-free risk.' Imagine entire portfolios that are striving to have only five percent returns in an environment when real-price inflation is the same or higher! The problem is most of the macro themes and ideas that protect real spending power are not well represented in mainstream media."

"So these themes and ideas are the financial soap operas you follow?"

"Yes, but it's not just these macro themes. These soap operas also offer an entirely different investment philosophy. We take only five or ten percent of our investment income with the objective to achieve two or three hundred or even a thousand percent with these ideas. You probably think this is crazy, don't you?"

"Sounds like gambling. You young bucks get lucky on some Internet stock or oil well discovery and think you're geniuses. I've seen how that movie ends, Johnny. It won't be long until you dribble your lucky score into big losses."

"You say I'm a gambler, I say I'm a calculated speculator—a contrarian investor, if you will. But if you want to use a gambling metaphor, that's fine. Let's look at the market as if it were a casino. I may be sitting at the blackjack table of investments with my higher risk positions, but what sets me apart from the crowd is that I'm able to count cards by using the tools and advice offered in my financial soap operas."

"So you admit it. You're gambling!"

"Let me put it another way; a rather more conservative method of articulating this point. Benjamin Graham, often considered the father of value investing, a man who was revered by other famous value investors such as Warren Buffett and Irving Kahn, once described the opportunities in markets the following way . . . I'll paraphrase, if I may?"

"You may indeed."

"Graham said that in the short term, markets act like voting machines, but in the long term, they act like weighing machines. In the short term, investors cast their votes by buying or selling stocks, causing them to behave highly irrationally in times of exuberance and/or in times of panic. That's why stocks can trade at dizzying multiples in the good times and crash below book value during times of crisis. In the long term, markets act like weighing machines as the true value of a solid investment always comes out. Sometimes it just takes time. This is sound value investing, and one can exploit the arbitrage, or the psychology between these two situations, to make a profit. It's a little bit more complicated than just buying low and selling high."

"Right, thus the saying 'buy when they cry and sell when they yell.'"

"Yup. Who doesn't know that one? When my barber's kid is giving me stock tips, it's definitely time to sell, and probably has been for a while. If you want to make a real profit in the markets, sometimes you need to disagree with the crowd. Isn't that the gist of investing—to be contrary? Otherwise, you're always buying the page-one story, which suggests that you are taking your position at the top or very near the top. I rarely ever invest in a story on page one—that's the familiar market where you or I can have little advantage. I prefer to invest in the story on page sixteen that is going to page one. There is a reason they call it a 'market,' as the person you are buying from or selling to clearly does not share the same investment strategy as you or maybe has missed something. If you know the what, when, or how, and they don't, that makes them a victim and you a contrarian who can profit from the advantage."

"Okay, I admit that's interesting, but you're talking to me like a common rube, Johnny. So not only should I be following my daily papers and financial shows for page-one stories, I should supplement the time I allocate by getting educated on broader page-sixteen themes and ideas?"

"Absolutely," Johnny replied. "Until you can see things in 360 degrees, you're still a passive investor. And I don't say that to discourage you; it's just a fact. Most passive investors panic when all hell breaks loose, becoming victims rather than exploiting a situation as a contrarian. If you don't follow your investments, sectors, and cycles like a soap opera—by that I mean every day, every week, and every month—then it's pretty hard to see the tide turning."

"Here's a question for you. How does the average guy in Oklahoma or Virginia find out about these things? We're talking about these themes and ideas, inflation and spending power, which is interesting. But what was your lucky break that led you to start following financial soap operas?"

"Well, Doc, as you know, back when I was working on your old house is about the time that I first started to dabble in the stock market and I ended up losing almost everything I put in. In the grand scheme of things, it wasn't much money, but at the time it felt like a small fortune. And it was also around that time I got my lucky break, if that's what we're going to call it."

"I can hardly wait to hear this."

"I was working on a project in a downtown office tower and while doing so, a big-shot investor—a real tycoon—took a liking to me. We would chit-chat about life, sports, our weekend recreations, and the most important theme for me—how to make real money. Point blank, I asked him how I could empower myself to be able to stop working nine-to-five. I wanted to be an investor like he was. He answered by taking out a pen and writing down five little sentences on the back of a napkin, which I framed long ago."

"What are they? I bet the first one was buy low and sell high. Ha!"

"You're good, Doc, but I think that's the kind of advice you pay a quarter for. Here they are, one to five. I'll write them down for you too."

He pulled a pen and small notepad out of his pocket and began scribbling. I was glad not to be getting a used napkin. Still, when he handed me the slip of paper, I read the five points carefully.

1. *If you pay peanuts, you get monkeys.*
2. *Don't invest in the story on page one, invest in the story on page sixteen that's headed to page one.*
3. *Get a passport and use it.*
4. *If you need a pencil and paper, it's too close to call.*
5. *Surround yourself with the smartest people in the world.*

After I looked up from the paper, he spent a few seconds covering each of the five points. He said it all boiled down to one simple piece of advice, but before he said what that was, he asked me to sum up what I'd learned without looking at the paper.

"Yesterday's news costs peanuts," I ventured, "so you shouldn't expect too much from it. And it makes total sense that you want to find great page-sixteen stories to invest in. So what's the advice that combines all five?"

"Follow high-quality, world-famous newsletter writers. Think about it, Doc. If I want suggestions on highly prospective, yet still unknown stories, where would I get them? Mainstream media doesn't often offer advice about specialized fields or cutting-edge ideas, nor do they offer real access to the leading experts related to them, do they?"

"So these newsletter writers source themes and ideas for their subscribers, that—let me guess—are so compelling that you don't need a pencil and paper to figure out the value proposition?"

"These are famous contrarian investors who are experts in their specific fields with documented track records and who have been around for ten, twenty, even forty years. They clearly lay out opportunities in a simple, straightforward manner and they know all the leading thinkers and famous players related to them, placing you right at the table, so to speak. On top of that, anyone with an Internet connection has the collected knowledge of mankind at their fingertips, meaning you can listen to, read, and enjoy interviews, essays, and speeches from almost anyone who has ever lived. Grasp the immensity of that! That's what he meant by surrounding yourself with the smartest people in the world. You may not have the opportunity to physically meet everyone, but due to the vastness of modern technology, you can learn about their ideas and hear what they had to say. However, you have to remain hyperaware and follow the content of your financial soap operas daily, weekly, and monthly—kind of like you would a Harlequin romance novel."

"My wife loved to watch those sappy romantic soap operas, but this is first time I've ever heard of them in reference to finance. I must say, that's a great way to explain how someone should stay current on anything they're directly connected to."

"A financial soap opera is the perfect analogy. How do you know the significance of an event or development if you're not current? It's the same in a soap opera. If you jump into the middle of a story that's been going on for months or years and watch one episode where a character gets killed, big deal. It means nothing to you because you have no context. But if you had been tuning in every day since the beginning, it would be hugely significant."

"Do you have a direct example relevant to investing?"

"Do you remember when the earthquake in Japan caused a tidal wave that destroyed the Fukushima Nuclear Plant?"

"Of course."

"It took a couple of days to fully grasp the gravity of that situation, but in the days, weeks, and months after the disaster, anything and everything that had even a smidgen to do with nuclear power or uranium mining got crushed. Point being, if you were not current, your pocketbook potentially got hurt real bad."

"All right, that makes sense. So if one had been following an expert in that field, as a soap opera, they would have been updated day to day, and made more aware?"

"Things happen in the world every day that affect investments positively and negatively. My goal, with the assistance of my specialized newsletters, is to try and figure out the trade winds that push opportunities up and down during a long-term trend and pounce on obvious market inefficiencies. In order to do that, I need to have an opinion, my own opinion, not a Xerox of someone else's, and it needs to be highly informed and well researched. I took the advice of the tycoon and subscribed to various newsletters and started to follow these expert writers, analysts, and just plain old famous investors. Some of these guys write weekly or monthly, some are cheap and some are crazy expensive. Collectively, they cover most investment classes—including how real inflation impacts every facet of our lives."

"So the five tips on the napkin were actually illustrating the necessity of subscribing to specialized newsletter writers," I said. "But the question is how did you find them in the first place? And how did you decide who was the best and what sectors to follow?"

"You're one step ahead of me, Doc. As I was scratching my head trying to put the five tips together, I asked the tycoon the same question. Funny, he was expecting me to ask that exact question and he provided a simple answer— if I was serious about upping my game, I would need to attend a world-class contrarian investment conference. The who's who would all be there for my accelerated due diligence."

"So, obviously, you went?"

"I sure did," Johnny replied. "I attended one of the most renowned—and expensive, I may add—conferences in the world. It was full of tech billionaires, politicians, and most of the famous newsletter writers who provide the financial soap operas. Over the four-day event, I was able to hear thirty of them speak and, even more importantly, I was able to talk with the ones who intrigued me. I also spoke to dozens— hell, I must have spoken to a hundred folks—about their past experiences with various writers, famous or otherwise. And then I was ready to take the plunge."

"So *that's* how you made enough money to buy a Porsche?"

"Kind of. You see, I am the most skeptical guy in the

world and I still didn't believe or trust some of their sugges-tions. I wanted to invest in things I knew intimately well. I started to document their ideas and, lo and behold, after one year and three thousand dollars in paid subscriptions—I told you they weren't cheap—I found that the writers I picked were up eighty percent on average with their ideas. If you can do the math, and I know you can, that outperformed almost any market or mutual fund."

"Well, in the 2008 financial crisis, it didn't matter what you owned. *Everything* went down, way down. There is no way you can tell me that you or any of your expert-advice newsletter writers saw that one coming!"

"When they raid the house of ill repute, they arrest everyone, including the piano player."

Johnny smiled as he said that, so I decided to ponder on it a moment before I replied.

"You're trying to say that when a total meltdown is happening, the good is thrown away with the bad?"

"The whole market went down. It was an all-asset-class sell-off affecting almost every single company on the board. Investors in droves sold otherwise solid stocks at throwaway levels. Fear had never been stronger than it was during that crisis. They clearly missed the memo the Chinese philosophers use: the deeper the crisis, the greater the opportunity. Rather than cry in your beer, that was the exact time to rebalance your devalued portfolio and pick up best-in-class investments that had been trashed beyond their book value. And *that* is just what we did."

"Okay, so give me an example."

"I'll tell you about a string of events I watched transpire from close range while following a suggestion from one of my newsletter writer friends. In the fall of 2008, there was a company that was trading at twenty-seven dollars a share, only to crash to four during the height of the meltdown.

The kicker was it had four dollars per share in cash, plus it had no debt and, most importantly, fifteen per share in paid facilities. It gets better. Even when those perceptive enough to recognize this opportunity started buying, it continued to fall to two dollars a share!"

"What? It had zero debt, four dollars a share in cash and fifteen a share in paid facilities, and it was trading fifty percent below cash in the bank?"

"Yup. The deeper the crisis, the greater the opportunity. Volatility, as we all remember, was at an all-time high, so as Graham used to preach, this created an unprecedented once-in-a-lifetime situation. The real underlying value in the long term, the weighing machine of value, was distorted by the short-term voting of terrified shareholders dumping their shares."

"So if I had been following this particular soap opera, I could have doubled my money?"

"Doubled? Didn't you just hear about the opportunity I explained? Remember when they raided the house of ill repute, even the piano player was arrested. This company was that piano player and it was soon realized that the long-term value proposition was the sum of the parts plus cash, which equated to nineteen dollars a share. Twelve months later, that company traded up to as high as eighteen! A nine hundred percent gain! Was that gambling, educated speculation, or, as I like to call it, contrarian investing? Or was it just plain old value investing and exploiting the difference between the short-term panic and the long-term underlying value?"

"Good example, but for someone my age, it still seems risky. Besides, there's nothing wrong with investing in steady staple stocks that, frankly speaking, are never going to zero. I don't want to get caught up with all the hoodlums and hyenas on Wall Street."

"You've been caught in the quagmire of extreme volatility that has been present for global investors this past decade or so. You're not the only one because it's a worldwide reality. We've all lost money and no investor alive has been immune to losses. What investors need to do is always reassess, rebalance, and accept the wisdom that, when the facts change, so must we."

"'When the facts change, I change my mind. What do you do, sir?'" I rattled off the famous quote attributed to John Maynard Keynes to show I was paying attention.

"Another bingo!" Johnny shouted. "It's also not wrong to be conservative as one grows old; you being twenty years older than me, it makes sense to reduce risk. That is why for someone like you, it's wise to have a totally diversified portfolio. Steady income is logical and the more speculative type of investments, *educated* speculation I mean, should also decrease as one nears retirement."

"Then if I don't need the stock tips, so to speak, I want to follow these soap operas to protect myself from other pitfalls like inflation and loss of real spending power?"

"Yes. That's the foundation to give you confidence in all aspects of your financial planning. However, I also feel that there can always be a responsible portion of one's portfolio allocated to well-researched contrarian investments to profit from the longest trend in history."

"Which is?"

"The ascent of man—more people consuming more things."

"So consumption is clearly one of the themes in your financial soap operas?"

"It's not simply consumption. I like to embrace specific subsectors that society can't live without. If there are going to be more people in the future, and I am pretty confident there will be, then what are those folks going to need?"

"And you have experts to help you find such subsectors?"

"Sure do. And I found them by participating in various conferences and being current on contrarian-themed newsletters, which are huge advantages very few average investors have. How many people do you know who will travel halfway across the country to attend an investment conference?"

"I wouldn't even know where to find the info if I wanted to. You got lucky with the tip from your tycoon friend and now I can consider myself lucky that you passed it on to me."

"Maybe I was lucky but the point is ninety-nine percent of the population is the same as you—too busy paying twenty-five cents to read page-one stories to even consider that there are alternatives. I've obtained so much valuable knowledge and advice and so many relationships from participating in these events that they have literally paid for themselves a hundredfold. If I never attended another event again, I would still have the legacy of all the tools on what to read and who to follow. With direct access to CEOs and other famous investors, I now have a lifetime of possibilities in furthering my education and, in turn, access to future investment opportunities."

"Okay, Johnny. I'll admit, this is all very interesting and I'll keep these five tips on my office desk. If I want to start my own financial soap opera, who do you recommend I follow?"

"Only you can answer that question because you have to invest in things you know and understand. But maybe I can help you narrow it down past maintaining real spending power. Too bad—it's going to have to wait 'til next Saturday."

Once again, we didn't get any actual work done. I began to come around to the idea that investing like a contrarian was, if nothing else, at least more interesting than my typical Baby Boomer ways. Johnny's ideas and passion for investing were infectious—you could see he had learned a lot from ten years as a participant. As I placed the small piece of paper on my desk, I couldn't help but wonder about number three on the list, the only one we didn't discuss. I had the funny feeling I was going to need a passport real soon.

The global shift

Johnny had hit me with a straight jab during our first Saturday together, racing away in a car I could likely afford but would never have the guts to actually go out and buy. In my circles, one had to be filthy rich to throw away so much hard-earned cash on such a vanity purchase.

Then he floored me again at our not-so-productive Saturday work session with a flurry of advice and insights on a different way to look at investments. I found myself counting down the seconds until our next meeting, even though it was only Tuesday. My skepticism as to how an electrician could find such an impressive level of financial independence had been put to rest by his demonstrated knowledge base and the tips he had received from various sources. If it worked for him, it could work for me, I thought. Since we'd last met, I put my renovation schedule into turbo overdrive.

I managed to finish tiling the entire bathroom over the weekend, then was able to strip the old flooring out of the kitchen in a single night. It was the only thing I could do really, as my mind was churning nonstop with ideas related to our talks.

If I were to become a participant rather than a passive investor, I needed to consider the point of our whole conversation. What sector or theme should I follow? Johnny told me that when you consider what to invest in, you should always keep close to your profession or expertise. Or put simply, "shoemaker, stick to your sole."

Perhaps I should become more familiar with life sciences or biotechnology, I thought, both of those being very important to Johnny's theme of "more people consuming more things." I started to wonder if he would meet me for dinner rather than wasting another Saturday in my half-finished kitchen? It couldn't hurt to ask.

I had to admit, there was an odd feeling about a middle-aged man calling up someone who is young enough to be his son to see if he can do a short-notice midweek dinner to talk about investing. I called him right away, before I could chicken out.

"What's up, Doc?" he joked, Bugs Bunny voice and all.

I laughed. As a doctor, I'd certainly had the line tossed out at me before, but usually it sounded forced. And usually, my response was an equally forced smile. This felt different, lighter and warmer, not someone trying to be funny and me trying to be polite, but more a friend catching you off guard. Were we that close already?

"Johnny, I've been thinking about our discussion about financial soap operas. I've got a couple of great ideas, and rather than waste another Saturday under the pretense of renovations, I was wondering if you'd like to grab a beer and bite instead? Maybe tomorrow?"

"Great idea. I see I've got the juices of due diligence boiling inside you."

"It's hard not to. You've turned some of my hardened beliefs upside down."

"Thursday, I could do a beer. Want to meet me at the Black Kamel? That trendy joint on Sixth and Main near the rail yards? Say, 7 p.m.?"

"The rail yards? You mean in that industrial part of town? Sure, I'll find it. Should I bring my laptop?"

"Not yet."

That was easy. For a young and successful guy, he sure had lots of spare time for me, and that's a good thing. It made sense to be efficient with my time, and his, and blowing another weekend with El Grande as our backdrop and not our focus would have been moronic.

• • •

A small point of pride: I've never been late in my life, nor have I ever pressed the snooze button, not even once. In the event of a traffic jam, it can happen to anyone, but I make sure to preempt such obstacles by always trying to arrive a little early. It's a strange little quirk that has worked so far, so no sense changing it.

When I saw Johnny's Porsche parked outside, I knew two things—I was at the right place and he'd beaten me here! As I walked into this trendy joint, which looked like it used to be an old butcher shop, I saw Johnny waiting for me over in the corner. It was a surprisingly packed room and most of the customers couldn't be a day over thirty. Scanning the room and surveying the tightness of everyone's jeans, I felt a bid odd navigating the room in my usual sweater-and-khakis combo. Johnny was equally out of place wearing what looked like a skintight cycling outfit.

"Doc! Over here!" Johnny yelled from across the bar.

Everyone craned their stylishly outfitted necks to stare at the fashion collision that was about to take place.

"Interesting place," I said as I sat down, ignoring the stares. "I don't think I've been to this part of town for the better part of ten years. It sure has changed."

"I'm just doing my part to gentrify the city. Now you can be a part of it too."

"Don't hold your breath. Sipping a latté in the corner of Starbucks is more my speed. I'm not sure what you mean by 'gentrify' anyways. I always seem to hear people protesting about it on the news."

"Some might try to make the case that you simply walking in here and having a cocktail is going to result in the displacement of lower-income residents and lead to skyrocketing rents."

"But let me guess, you've got an alternative opinion on the subject?" I asked.

"Any neighborhood in which a dive bar can attract the patronage of a wealthy doctor like yourself is doing something very right."

"But I only came here because you picked the spot."

"It doesn't matter. Now that you're here, you'll be back. Trust me."

Something behind me caught Johnny's eye. When I turned to look, I discovered two profoundly attractive young women walking towards us, a blonde and a brunette, each carrying what looked to be tubes of rolled-up foam. They were svelte and healthy, also dressed in skintight outfits, though with tight T-shirts worn over their tops. Each had wires running from their hips and ending at earbuds draped around their necks. They looked like a Betty and Veronica for the 21st century.

"Doc, may I introduce my yoga partners? Meet Tammy and Jenny."

"Yoga? Wow, of course. Now I understand your goofy outfit, Johnny."

Both women smiled at that. I smiled back.

"Nice to meet you, ladies."

"I forgot my slacks and sweater back at Harvard," the blonde said.

"Don't tease the doc, Jenny. He's just afraid we might catch a cold," the brunette laughed.

"Why don't I treat the namaste gang to a high-calorie, high-carb glass of goodness?"

They sat down with us and began examining the mile-long beer list as if it was second nature to them. Gazing at the stunning yoga twins scanning the drink options, it was hard not to get motivated.

"So you all do yoga?" I ventured.

"Yoga feeds the soul, Doc. How else do you think I'm able to keep this svelte Swedish teenager's body?"

The waitress came up beside us, simply cocking her head rather than asking if we were ready to order. She was also young and healthy and seemed to have features from various backgrounds. She first seemed European, but when I turned to the list of beers, from the corner of my eye she appeared East Asian. I didn't question it, focusing instead on the pressure I was feeling to make a choice fast.

Jenny asked the waitress something about Germany and chose a wheat beer.

"If I'm going to do gluten, might as well go all the way," she laughed.

Tammy checked if another beer was from South Africa or just a South African style. I didn't hear the answer, but she ordered it.

Johnny ordered an India Pale Ale, with some other specifications I didn't hear. I put my menu down, giving up.

"I'll have that, too," I said.

The waitress scribbled on her notepad, smiling.

"I'll be right back, guys," she said as she spun around and skated her way through the crowd.

"Thanks, Amalia," called out Tammy.

I was amazed. I knew that Gen Xers didn't live in my world, but I hadn't realized how different their world was. Beyond the outfits and the ever-present wires, they didn't have a regular drink order. There was also the casual comfort with the waitress, whose name they even knew!

"You know the waitress?" I asked Tammy. "Amalia, is it?"

"We all know Amalia," she answered. "She's sweet."

"She's been promising to teach me some Hungarian dance," Jenny said. "I saw her do it with her troupe once. It looks so beautiful."

"She's Hungarian?" I asked. "Well, that explains the name."

"Well, half-Hungarian," Johnny answered. "And half-Thai."

"Do you all know her from yoga?"

"Just from here," Jenny said, staring off into the crowd. "And she's already coming back with our drinks!"

"Best waitress ever," Tammy smiled at me.

Amalia was at our table in no time, doling out our drinks. It hit me that not only was this generation's world different, it was so much bigger than mine. They'd dropped the names of different countries while ordering beer, where I would go to restaurants expecting that everything would be from the same country and that country would be named on the door of the establishment. They practiced Indian exercises and tried dances from Eastern Europe. They thought nothing of Amalia's rather unique heritage.

"So, Doc," Jenny asked, sipping her beer, "you don't do yoga?"

"Uh, no. Well, my daughter's tried to get me to, but I never did."

I sipped my beer, so I wouldn't have to further explain. I was recognizing that I was the outsider, not just here, but in my lack of connection to so much of the world. I was starting to get a better idea of Johnny's worldview.

"You should come to a class with us," Tammy smiled.

"We go every Thursday. Come with us next time," Jenny purred. "We'll take ten pounds off your frame if you give us a month."

"You'd love it, Doc," Johnny urged.

"Also, you should be suggesting yoga to all your patients," suggested Tammy. "I teach classes. Here's my card. We'll hook you up with a deal."

Ah! So this wasn't just a casual meeting. Tammy had a good business sense.

"Well, I'm sold. If you gals get a commission for this, I'm guessing you must do very well."

I felt a twinge of embarrassment as Jenny mouthed the word "gals" to Tammy.

"Huge trend, Doc, huge trend," Johnny offered, obviously amused by the scene. "And you should never get in the way of a trend. A trend is like a parade—it's very hard to create one but when they're underway, you want to be tuned in. Recognizing patterns is what following your soap opera is all about. These girls right here, for example. They're tastemakers. You could even call them influencers. What they're wearing today will directly correspond with where the trend goes tomorrow. Remember how Lululemon stock performed as the yoga craze took off?" Johnny asked me, standing up.

"No, but something tells me I wish I had."

"Oh, I think it's time for business talk," Jenny teased.

"You two want some space, Johnny?" Tammy asked.

"Yeah, we should probably shift gears. But you two stay here. I reserved a booth for me and Doc in the back," Johnny replied. "Tell Amalia your drinks are on my tab."

As we said goodbye to the Betty and Veronica look-alikes, I glanced around the rest of the room and started to wonder if it was even safe to park my car in this neighborhood. I could only trust that if Johnny was confident enough to leave his Porsche outside, I'd just have to trust for the best.

"So this is where you spend your free time?"

"The best way I can put it is by saying that if you were to go to dinner with a group of only doctors or only bankers or only any exclusive group, how boring is that? My definition of a great dinner, and of a great social life in general, is to be surrounded by every facet of society. That means artists, gardeners, business guys, you name it. Try organizing an eclectic dinner for twelve sometime—that's what places like this represent to me."

"*Touché.* I just don't get out too much anymore."

"Even the late Ray Charles could see that, Doc. That's why I don't have a problem grabbing some chow with you and talking about soap operas. Just don't tell my yoga partners what we were chatting about when you see them in class," Johnny chuckled.

As I laughed off his comments, I thought about the best way to approach our upcoming conversation. I wanted to put myself into the arena with a solid base. Even though I was impressed with Johnny's insights, they were still unclear at that point, and besides, I'd been investing for thirty years. While it was true he seemed to have far more freedom than I, it wasn't my fault that I loved my work as a family doctor and had never really been into exotic travel.

"I've been putting a lot of thought into getting a little more involved in following some of these more specialized sectors," I said. "And for me, the most sensible thing would be something that pertained to my career."

"Naturally."

"Life sciences and biotechnology have been relevant for decades. Plus, there's lots of capital for health. Society in general wants to live longer and healthier and there is always an increasing investor-appetite for such things. That much I've learned from all those hours watching business TV."

"Great start. So what now?"

"I was going to ask you."

"About biotechnology?"

"Yes. Do you know any respected analysts or newsletter writers who specialize in biotech?"

"I'm not a biotech guy. I don't follow that soap opera."

"What? That's not what you said last Saturday. You said that you went to world-class conferences and met the best of the best. You were able to meet all these investors and ask them which newsletter writers they subscribed to, right? So shouldn't you have met some biotech specialists?"

"Only if you pick the right conference."

"The right conference?"

"Different horses for different courses, Doc."

"So you can't recommend a straightforward way to get more involved in a sector I want to follow as a financial soap opera? Now I'm confused. Just spell it out for me. What are you, Johnny the electrician, investing in right now? Besides inflation and guarding your spending power, what financial soap operas are you following?"

"Like I said, I'm following the longest trend in history."

"The ascent of man, more people consuming more things?"

"Yup. I try to follow all the themes that can have an impact on more people consuming more things. But when it comes to actual investments, I've been investing in the same theme for the past decade. And this theme will be valid, in my opinion of course, for the next ten, even twenty years."

"That being?"

"I follow, and I mean I religiously follow, the single largest migration of human beings in the history of the world, and I plan on gloriously profiting from it."

"Is that a real sector or a cute title for some kind of exchange-traded mutual fund?"

"Funny, Doc. I already told you that the longest trend in history is the ascent of man. That's a fact that no one can deny. Right now, there are one hundred million people having sex."

"Right. So you follow population growth? Reproductive technology? The prophylactic industry?"

"Boy, it's going to take me a few minutes to explain this one, but yes, population growth is one of the pillars. However, a better word to describe what I'm talking about is demographics."

"Okay, I'm going to get my pen and paper out for this one. Are you going to hit me with an encyclopedia of facts?"

"I've got plenty of opinions, but you know what they say about opinions, so yeah, let's just stick to the facts. The overarching theme that can help any investor understand a changing world is to fully appreciate the power of shifting demographics and grasp how that will affect everything around us."

"How is this going to help me follow my own financial soap opera in a sphere that I understand?"

"The cornerstone of your newfound interest in investing should be to fundamentally know who will be the 'bulge' of whatever you're going to follow. The world has changed, and if you haven't accepted that, then that's where you need to start."

Just as I was getting excited to start my new journey into financial bliss, Johnny slams the brakes upon take off. Demographics? Population growth? How the world has changed? Last time I checked, I was on top of China, Brazil, and the developing world—and yes, I understood that there was a shift taking place on a global scale. But how was this going to affect my interest in following life sciences or biotechnology?

"So what you're talking about is growth in China and the developing world?" I asked.

"The story of China's rise has been well publicized, and I'm quite sure you've heard from all the bulls and all the Sino-bears when you watch TV or read your papers, right?"

"It's been talked about almost daily for as long as I can remember. And for the record, that theme is a page-one story, Johnny."

"That's true. But have you been to China, Doc?"

"No. Why would I?"

"Have you been to Russia? Brazil? Indonesia? Africa?"

"You already know the answer to that. No, I haven't. But that's not going to make me an expert anyway now, is it? I've been to Tijuana and I can't speak a lick of Spanish or tell you anything about Mexican macroeconomics."

"There is an old saying, 'it's easier to see once than to hear a hundred times.' Never was that more relevant to me than on my first train ride across China. And I wasn't staying in Beijing or Shanghai either. It was Tianjin. That's where I first got my mind blown at the sheer level of economic activity. Have you even heard of Tianjin before, Doc?"

"No, I haven't, but I'm eager to know why it was so mind-blowing."

"Some basic facts first—Tianjin is the fourth-largest city in China, located in the north on the Yellow Sea. The metropolitan population is around fourteen million, and it's just one of many megacities in China. When I was there, I saw more economic activity, overhead cranes I mean, than you could find anywhere in the United States, and I had never even heard of the place before I went!"

"Hold it right there. The overbuilding of China has been well documented and the fact that there was lots of development is nothing new. The real question is what is the hangover from this construction boom going to look like? My guess is ugly and two Advils in the morning are going to do squat."

"Doc, during the eighteen hundreds, France became more urban than agrarian, a feat that had taken hundreds of years to achieve. Later, the same thing occurred in the United States and it took about a hundred years. In both of those examples, their populations were previously eighty percent rural and twenty percent urban—now, they are the exact opposite. Only in 2012 did China cross the halfway mark—just over fifty percent of that humongous and growing population is just now living in an urban setting. Picture that, Doc—there are still six or seven hundred million citizens in China who have yet to participate in basic progress."

"But that will take another hundred years to actualize."

"Not so. While it's true it happened in a century in the US, in China and elsewhere in the developing world, it's happening in just a few decades. China's first migration wave of three hundred million people took place over the past thirty years—the fastest industrial revolution in history. With the pace of change taking place around us and the speed at which information travels, there is no army, no government, and no spiritual force that can hold these people back. You can write *that* down on your little notepad."

"Got it," I said, scribbling. "There is no army, no government, and no spiritual force that can hold these people back."

"Not only are global citizens becoming consumers like you and me at a faster pace than ever before in recorded history, overall world population is growing at unprecedented levels. It's estimated that the population of the world will be an astonishing nine billion people by 2050. While it's true that birth rates have dropped in many countries around the world, what we're talking about is the next wave of one billion people that will join us in the consumer economy in the coming decade. This is the demographic shift of consumerism I'm talking about and it will affect every sector. So these patterns deserve to be appreciated and fully understood."

"What about the ghost cities I've read about?" I asked.

"If you build it, they will come. In the fifties, the United States built her interstate highways, the largest public works project in the world at that time. Before that, countless other great infrastructure projects were built across the 9.8 million square kilometers (about six million miles) of the United States. If anyone wonders about building ghost cities, they need not look any further than right here in the good old USA, a country forged on ambitious build-first megaprojects."

The enthusiasm and positivity with which Johnny was spilling out all these facts was impressive. I suppose I had become rather cynical toward China's explosive growth, a side effect of the twenty-four-hour business news cycle. He had used the phrase "like reading a Harlequin romance novel" to describe how one should follow micro and macro themes, and he was clearly an expert on China, one of his economic soap operas.

As I looked around this funky little bar he had brought me to, I started to pinpoint examples of the points he was driving at. But did anyone here know what was going on in our world? These twentysomethings knew plenty about social media and what their friends had for breakfast, but were they following any page-sixteen news stories? Did they know the price of even a single commodity?

I was reminded of the first cell phone I ever used, a giant, hulking beast that burned your ear off if you talked too long. It was pretty much useless and the reception was terrible.

"Oddly enough, China at 9.6 million square kilometers, or about 6 million square miles, is basically the same size as the United States, but with five times the population—that's 1.3 billion citizens," Johnny continued. "Can you imagine that in rural China, there is still the population equivalent of two United States who have yet to achieve basic living standards? Even more importantly, tens of millions of people are making the pilgrimage from a rural existence to an urban one. Have you seen how that movie ends before?" he said.

"You mean the France and US examples."

"It's a global phenomenon. It happens in economy after economy after economy. It's no coincidence that populations usually settle out when approximately eighty percent of the citizens live in an urban setting."

"What about ghost cities? You still haven't addressed that."

"When I hear stories of 'overbuilding' in China, I consider the demographic shift that has been happening for only thirty years. Let me illustrate this even more vividly. Imagine that you were going to relocate the entire population of the United States, all three hundred-plus million people, to the Eastern Seaboard from Boston to Miami. Imagine that you needed to fortify all that infrastructure and that you had to do it in thirty years . . ."

"I'd say you're crazy and that you couldn't do it, but then I know that is precisely what has happened in China."

"That's exactly what they have done since the late seventies and will continue doing for the coming decades. Who actually lives in China, demographically speaking that is, from a technical statistics point of view?"

"No clue, please fill me in."

"There are four major generational blocks of people. The Cultural Revolution generation totals about 160 million; they are fifty-five to sixty-five years old and run the country for the most part. Only one million of them are college graduates. Then there are about 210 million Lucky Risers, those that are forty-five to fifty-five years old, five million of which are college graduates. Third are the PC Generation, 220 million people, with eight million being college grads."

"So who's left?" I inquired, bracing myself for what was obviously going to be a shocking final data point.

"Ah, the millennials," Johnny whispered, just loud enough for me to hear it clearly.

"Millennials?" I replied. "You mean the twenty-somethings?"

"There are four 415 million people in China between the ages of sixteen and thirty-five, and well over 100 million of them have already graduated from college. Most of them have a smartphone, and they know exactly how the world works. Remember, anyone with an Internet connection has the collected knowledge of mankind at their fingertips!"

All I could think to myself was *wow*. I knew that the United States had just over three hundred million citizens, and I knew Western Europe also had about the same number. The context of the actual demographics was a game changer, to say the least. In my mind, I had been using the term Gen Xer to visualize younger generations, but culturally interwoven to them were these millennials. Anyone from the age of sixteen to forty, on a global scale, was going to have far greater expectations when endowed with the power of the Internet.

"Eighty percent of these millennials were born rurally," Johnny continued. "Now the majority live in cities. There are only about 350 million working-age people in the US and Europe combined!" Johnny exclaimed.

"Let me guess: The millennials—and Gen Xers, for that matter—are not that interested in working in factories anymore?"

"Well, would you? When you use common sense, it's clear that they don't want blue-collar jobs. Nor, if they have a college degree, do they have any interest in being factory workers. One of the main reasons China's economy is shifting to a consumer-based 'demand economy' is these overwhelming demographic realities from these new consumers. Who is going to stop these citizens from making the greatest migration in the history of the world?"

"Let me guess: There is no army, no government, and no spiritual force that can stop them . . ."

"Can they, Doc?"

"You keep saying this started a few decades ago. What happened?"

"If you could point to a single person who unleashed this Asian dragon, it would be Deng Xiaoping, who took over the Chinese economy in 1979. Since then there has been almost ten percent annual GDP expansion as he encouraged the entrepreneurial spirit of his people to run wild. Prior to Deng, the Chinese were locked in the Maoist disasters of the Great Leap Forward and the Cultural Revolution. Picture this: in 1979 there were only sixty privately owned vehicles in China! Sixty! From the time of Christ to the early eighteen hundreds, China had been the world's economic powerhouse. The Chinese were only taking a nap the past two hundred years and now are reclaiming their traditional position. How can anyone argue with 1.3 billion incredibly industrious people?"

"Only sixty privately owned cars? Are you sure?"

"It's a sad reality. China was incredibly backward just after the Mao regime. However, in the past thirty years, China has spent eight or nine percent of its GDP on infrastructure. No other country in the world has done that, and, coincidentally, their economy has grown by eight or nine percent annually. In the fifties, sixties, and seventies, the

United States used to spend four percent or more of GDP on infrastructure and the economy grew by, guess what, four percent or more. Now, we spend two percent of GDP on infrastructure and what has our growth rate been?"

"Two percent?"

"The Chinese are building it, and people from rural areas are migrating to the cities. And the cultural differences between Europe and America are hugely significant, but they are even greater for China."

"Give me an example."

"The very symbols of culture, the arts and the grand houses where it takes place, were always built in Europe by governments, often socialist ones, for their most entitled citizens. In America, there was always civic duty or specific philanthropic initiatives that built many of the great museums and bastions of culture. Whereas in China's planned economy, they think on the grandest scale possible, in ambitious five-year plans that lay out entire cities for future inhabitants. This is unprecedented in human history."

"Johnny, I'm not going to argue this point. It's a lot of people and the growth is mind-boggling, but the vast majority, even if they are moving to cities, are still very poor."

"Let's talk about poverty for a minute—and I need to credit Bill and Melinda Gates for a fantastic essay they wrote that addressed three myths regarding the world's poor. Myth number one was that poor countries are doomed to stay poor. They argue that they are not, and I have to agree with them. Considering that the Gateses are bequeathing most of their wealth, and that of Warren Buffett, to fight poverty, I think they can be acknowledged as being authorities on the subject of progress in developing countries. They predict that by 2035, there will be almost no poor countries left in the world. There will always be a few unhappy examples held back by politics or war, but by then, more than seventy percent of the world will have higher per-person incomes than China in the mid-2010s, which is already a meaningful number."

"What's myth number two?"

"Myth number two about the poor is that foreign aid is a big waste. Sure, it's true there is small-scale corruption, but the vast majority of funds are actually fixing major problems. The overwhelming evidence points to the fact that more and more people are living healthier, longer lives. A baby born in 1960 had an 18 percent chance of dying before her fifth birthday. Today, it's less than 5 percent. In 2035, it will be 1.6 percent. That's a tremendous amount of progress in only seventy-five years, so imagine the implications as we approach nine billion people in the near future.

"Finally, myth number three is that saving lives leads to overpopulation."

"That's a rather relevant point with respect to the soap opera that I intend on following."

"Let's look at the facts from their essay—as life expectancy rises, societies start to have fewer children. Falling death rates actually lead to falling birth rates, as happier, healthier families don't need to have so many children. We've already seen this happen across every culture in every corner of the planet. So saving lives does not lead to overpopulation. Population growth, the longest trend in history, has been a natural occurrence."

"The longest trend in history being the ascent of man," I said.

"Another bingo. Whether that changes past 2050 due to falling birth rates will not affect the financial decisions I make in the next five to ten years. It took just over twenty years for the last five hundred million people to be lifted out of poverty. What may surprise you is that it took a hundred years for the five hundred million before them. How long will it take for the next five hundred million? Perhaps only the next decade, which is within my investment time horizon and a blink of the eye for any investor with a similar medium-term horizon. And then what happens when those five hundred million people leave poverty? They start consuming *stuff* like you and I. Any way you slice it, there will be more people consuming more things and that is the overarching theme that every investor should follow because where is all the *stuff* going to come from?"

"You're learning all these facts about human progress on the Internet, right? How are you sure they can be verified?"

"The Internet is an incredible resource for so much up-to-date information. And yes, there is lots of misleading or simply false information in the mix. To buffer myself, I rely on the hard work and research of leading philanthropists like the Gateses and other critical thinkers."

"As you might guess, I'm not a big web surfer but bookmarking cool websites that provide great content seems both practical and important for objective decision making."

"Bill Gates has been very vocal, stating that he wants people to spread the word about alleviating poverty. His blog, *gatesnotes*, has a treasure trove of facts, opinions, and interactive videos that offer real solutions and logical insights on the topic."

"That is something that has always confused and bothered me. The diametrically opposed views of various groups and organizations, obviously biased, are impossible to change, no matter with what facts they are presented."

"Would it not then seem intelligent to have a flexible opinion? The single biggest benefit from following those like Bill Gates is the unbiased solution-based education they wish to provide to millions of readers around the world. Personally, I don't want to be dictated to as to what is right or wrong for my family; nor would someone on the other side of the planet. No matter how you slice it, the umbilical cord of human progress was, is, and will be *energy*! When we have the same per-person energy consumption as someone in Africa, then we can give them advice as to what they can and cannot have, not before!"

"'Umbilical cord of human progress'—I like that one, Johnny. I would think that most tolerant people want to form their own opinions. And as for mandating what level of modernization someone in Africa should have, I fully agree: They can strive for the future they deserve."

"Here is a profound statistic about energy consumption in Africa. A typical American refrigerator uses as much electricity in a year as nine Ethiopians!"

It was a shocking insight. At that moment, I realized just how drastically the world had changed—and is continuing to change. The immensity of what was transpiring began to set in: what used to take a century now took place in just a decade. I suppose I had fashioned a comfortable Boomer cocoon for myself over the past years that had insulated me from all this rapid change. The more I heard Johnny break things down, the more relevant it began to feel. I knew that I wanted to become a participant.

I'd never even once considered the implications of the *stuff* he talked about, nor the immense importance of energy. And there it was, all around us, in the food we were eating, the building we sat in, or glowing in the hands of every person in this bar.

We were living in a world where technology was advancing at breakneck speed throughout every moment of our lives. Most of the people in the room weren't even aware of the preceding era where old fogies like me had spent years fumbling around with outmoded technology like near-useless car phones and, before that, rotary phones.

The progress that almost every twenty- and thirty-something person around the world experienced was fluid and natural, to a point where giant leaps were completely ordinary—you could even say they were entitled to them. It truly makes you reconsider the headline-grabbing data points that have always proliferated in the media. This data may be financial nectar for PhD candidates, but front-page headlines could never derail the undeniable progress being achieved around the world.

It was refreshing to be reminded that some of the wealthiest people were unselfishly dedicating their lives to improving the lives of others. By providing every citizen in the world the tools to generate their own views, they were also proclaiming the world had changed. We should all appreciate and respect that reality.

Stuff comes with
an electrical cord

A week had passed since Johnny and I last met and, in the interim, I had successfully established base camp in El Grande. To get my house in order, both literally and figuratively, I first sold the outmoded automation system on Craigslist. It was the first time I'd ever used the website and, to my surprise, it was a fun experience. I'd definitely taken it on the chin in terms of recouping my investment, but the money was irrelevant as it had already been wasted. The point was to modernize.

Through a few hours of research on the web, I discovered a series of nifty automation systems that seemed surprisingly easy to set up. There were little self-contained units that plugged into outlets so you could automatically make coffee before you woke up, automatic window blinds, voice-activated thermostats, and a basketful of other gizmos and goodies. There was even an app that worked with your refrigerator to automatically notify you when you ran out of eggs. After sketching out a plan to futurize my house, I settled on a fancy lighting system that was controlled exclusively through a smartphone app. I was excited to show off my newfound tech-savvy when Johnny arrived for our next meeting at exactly 8 a.m. as planned. He was never late. I admired that about him because it demonstrated reliability and reminded me of myself.

"Good morning, Doc. Cappuccino?" he asked. "I thought you would appreciate some gourmet brew for a change."

"Now you're going to tell me even my coffee tastes are outdated?" I chuckled.

As he passed me the cup, I guided him to the kitchen where I had already installed a full set of the new lightbulbs.

"Here. Let me set the mood a little," I said, whipping out my phone.

I loaded up the app that enabled me to fade the lights from a bright white to a warm candescent yellow.

"Wow. Nice lights. How'd you swing that?"

"It was actually quite straightforward. These are smart lights, so smart even a Boomer like myself could figure them out."

"Look at you. In just over a week, you've gone from the Ahab of obsolete wiring systems to a tech geek."

"After our discussion on this great migration we've been talking about, I've put some thought into the implications of it all."

"Awesome. Glad to see you're really absorbing all this info."

"Let's talk a little about the sheer magnitude of this shift and consider for a moment if these people start buying *stuff* like we talked about. When I went out and bought the stuff needed to make my home automation dream a reality, I pondered a bit about that. Then, there was our talk about the ingredients in a Big Mac, which is also *stuff*. Shouldn't that be something to follow in terms of a financial soap opera?"

"Stuff, well, *stuff* is everywhere," Johnny said as he looked around the room. "These lights of yours are indeed *stuff*, very advanced stuff, but stuff nonetheless. But here's the question—when was the last time you were hungry, or thirsty, or in need of shelter?"

"Well, obviously . . ."

"It's okay, Doc. Trick question. My point is that once a group of people make the move from rural to urban, from peasant to worker and on to consumer, their way of life changes. Subsistence disappears from their vocabulary and their lives begin to revolve around the three Cs: comfort, convenience, and communication. And in order to achieve any of those things, it takes a whole lot more stuff than ever before. We get a dishwasher to free up time and a television to waste it. We get an air conditioner to stay cool and a heater to stay warm. Then later on, we get other luxuries like solar panels on our roofs and newer, more modern cars. When a society achieves their very own consumer revolution, as China and the developing world are undergoing right now, life becomes less about *needs* and more about *wants*. With an unprecedented number of new consumers, these luxuries need way more stuff to make them possible. All that stuff up here comes from down there," Johnny said, pointing to the ground.

"Wait. The stuff down there?"

"Where do you think everything comes from? Everything around you was either grown or mined! Commodities make everything around us possible. The question is—who's responsible for providing it to us?"

"Okay, I get it. Steel, concrete, lumber, food, whatever. It comes from the earth."

"Remember when we were in your office, I said I was the luckiest guy in the world? Well, I was so lucky that I won a lottery three times. By coincidence!"

"You son of a . . . Okay, okay, so that's how you did it! Why didn't you just tell me you're a lottery winner? Three wins? Johnny, that's incredible Are you pulling my leg?"

"Relax, Doc. I don't literally mean that I won the Publishers Clearing House prize or the state lottery. What I do mean is that I was endowed with being born in exactly the right place, at precisely the right time, and by luck or chance, I chose the ultimate profession to make me appreciate the gravity of the greatest migration of human beings in the history of the world."

"I have heard some tall tales in my time, sonny, but I have to say that one may take first prize. What in the name of sweet molasses are you talking about? Because you chose to become an electrician in the Pacific Northwest, and because it occurred in the early nineties, you think you won three lotteries? You're going to have to spell that one out for me."

"Have you read Malcolm Gladwell's brilliant book *Outliers*? You could say I was an outlier of sorts. But let me explain . . ."

"That was an amazing book. How are you going to weave your three lottery wins into being an outlier? I'm all ears."

"First of all, an outlier, as you know, describes people who are experts in their respective fields, people who 'stick out.' Most of these folks have had over ten thousand hours of experience, and many of them were born at the right place at the right time, like that pilot who landed the plane in the Hudson River. He had over ten thousand hours of experience. Or the Beatles, who not only had ten thousand hours of musical experience, they were also at the right place at the right time."

"So how do you fit in?"

"In the nineties, North America went through a technological revolution. Most of the great technology companies of our time were founded in Seattle and San Francisco in the seventies and eighties, but it wasn't until the nineties that they began to flourish. All these new technologies went into overdrive as governments around the world started deregulating their telecommunication sectors, and at the same time, the computer age started to take off in earnest. It was then that almost every homeowner in the developed world would buy their first real personal computer."

"When Windows '95 was released, I was one of those suckers lining up at the mall hours early to get my copy. It was the same year I bought Microsoft stock actually," I said.

"Not only did the computer revolution take place through the nineties and beyond, the wireless communications build-out accelerated. Who owned a cell phone in 1990?"

"Barely anyone."

"And who had one in the year 2000?"

"Everyone, including some rather annoying ten-year-olds in my neighborhood."

"Who built all that infrastructure? Where did cell phones work? Just as this telecommunications expansion build-out was accelerating, what we call the World Wide Web or the Internet exploded. And as you know, it's often acknowledged that Seattle is one of the capitals of the Internet age."

"Of which everyone in the Pacific Northwest is extremely proud."

"We sure are. And anyone who was born in the early to mid-seventies was graduating college in the early to mid-nineties, right? You see what I'm saying about the right place and the right time?"

"Okay, so you happened to be working in a field where you got to witness that take place, but what does that have to do with *stuff*, as you put it? I'm having a hard time seeing how the electrician part can be likened to winning a lottery or being an outlier."

"That was the biggest lottery score of all. While it's true thousands of people found great jobs in these various fields in Seattle, Silicon Valley, and elsewhere, only an electrician, who implemented both ends of the technology, could see the double opportunity. You see, living directly in between Seattle, a world capital of technology, and Vancouver, a world capital of the providers of *stuff*, this electrician could put it all together to connect the dots, A to Z."

"You've lost me now, Johnny. What's Vancouver got to do with *stuff*? What stuff exactly are we talking about now?"

"I mean commodities—what software and technology are to Seattle and San Francisco is what commodities, the building blocks of *stuff*, are to Vancouver, a world capital of companies who look for and provide commodities to end users."

"Okay, that makes sense. You mean the headquarters of these commodity companies are located in Vancouver. But let's finish the significance of you winning the lottery three times."

"Stick with me. Between 1992 and 2002, I did many things as an electrician. I was not your average sparky. I installed and re-installed *stuff* in telecommunication rooms, for Internet companies, wireless companies, anything that needed a wire in it. In the midst of all this crazy overtime, which was being financed by investors like yourself, I spent an entire summer touring beautiful British Columbia. And this is when I had the eureka moment that would change the course of my life."

"Let me guess. You realized you hated being an electrician?"

"Not even close. My work partner and I were on the top of a mountain in the absolute middle of nowhere. It took one and a half hours to traverse a logging road to reach this tiny, remote enclave of technology. A small outpost of the future set against the backdrop of wild rugged mountains and forest. We had visited dozens of similar sites that summer when suddenly it hit me."

"What happened? A bear jumped out of the woods? An eagle shat on your head?"

"Real funny. The eureka moment was that the entire planet was wireless, or would become so very soon. We were a hundred kilometers (about sixty miles) from the nearest town and you could surf the Internet or call your grandmother in rural India for a few pennies. And it was all possible from the comfort of a climate-controlled shelter. This expansion of technology happened in just a few short years, so what was going to happen in the next five years? Or the next ten? Over the course of the next generation? And most importantly, what was going to make it all possible?"

"Okay, so it happened fast. Are you trying to say it caught everyone off guard? The dot-com bomb happened pretty damn fast as well. What's your point?"

"The speed of technology is making things duplicate, triplicate, and expand in record speed. It's cheaper to fly across the world than ever before and it's almost free to make long-distance calls anywhere, anytime. We are in the most thrilling period of human history, one in which we are witnessing many technologies double every eighteen months! Imagine if we took away every smartphone, iPad, the Internet, all your email. This would put us back to the dark ages of 1990! Computer power is replacing brainpower and the full magnitude of this efflorescence of mankind is still unknown. If we use history to shed some light on another cosmic shift that affected humanity just over a century ago, what was the significance of industrial power replacing muscle power— like when automobiles replaced horses?"

History has always been a preoccupation of mine, right down to the books I read and through the phases of TV programming I watch. In my earlier years, it had been sports, then my stint with the home improvement fad, and lately I'd been fixated with watching business shows. But the two constants have always been my beloved Seattle Mariners and history. I also firmly believe that history does repeat itself, and the link between accelerated information transfer and advancing technology went hand in hand. Everything happened very fast these days and I was not up to speed. I was being exposed as a technological dinosaur.

"I get it," I said. "This wireless revolution is the 21st century equivalent to how the telegraph and telephone accelerated information transfer at the turn of the 20th century by a quantum leap."

"Yes, but it's way deeper than that. Let's use another example in history to see how fast technology changes and the aftermath that results. If you were born in the year 1900, imagine the progress you would have witnessed. Flight, cars, freeways, a man on the moon, the cellular phone! In 1903, the Wright brothers flew the first airplane and by the time World War I ended in 1918, each army had vast fleets of air weapons. After the first mass-produced automobile was built, it took Henry Ford only a decade to perfect the assembly line. His factories were then able to produce an automobile in only ninety-three minutes."

"Even a hundred years ago, technology was doubling in a single decade."

"In 1900, at the World's Fair in Paris, electricity was show-cased to demonstrate how it could make our lives easier. During the early part of the twentieth century, the whole world became electrified. This spawned an industrial boom in America, Europe, and around the world that has not stopped for one moment to this very day. A hundred years ago, technology could change top-to-bottom in a decade. Now, it can happen in eighteen months or less, and all of it needs an electrician to make it possible. Let's once again consider the phone, an invention that first hit the market at the turn of the 20th century. In only a generation, it evolved from a clunky thing that hung on a wall into the world's favorite, most indispensable, and versatile gadget—a technological marvel so brilliant that we never turn it off and always have it by our sides. Think about it, your smartphone's computer is more powerful than the one that powered the Apollo space mission!"

"Change happens at hyperspeed, I get that, and it makes sense that investors should follow change, but we're getting a little bit off-topic here. You still haven't finished the point from your eureka moment. I'm getting the idea that choosing to become an electrician was the most important of your so-called three lottery wins due to the fact that all these things need an electrician to function."

"That's what I'm saying, Doc. As I sat on that mountain-top and as the revelation of this massive change washed over me, all the dots connected to form the foundation of my future. All this *stuff*, whether it was a *want* or a *need*, had an electrical cord sticking out of it. Thirty years ago, the average US household had only a few electronic gizmos. Today, there are twenty, thirty, or more things that we all have that don't work unless they are plugged in or powered up. The same could be said for the developing world, when people go from a rural existence to an urban one, they automatically become electrified."

"That's why energy is the umbilical cord of human progress. But you're specifically talking about China here, right?"

"Not just, but it's the big one. The average household in China is also going to have twenty or so of these 'needs' and 'wants.' And there is only upside in the fact that the average American uses as much electricity to chill their beers as nine Ethiopians."

I immediately got a mental picture of people around the world being given the choice between a cold beer and a warm one. Of course they were going to want the cold one, just like we Americans did.

"Statistics tell us," Johnny continued, "that a fully urbanized home in China, Thailand, Mexico, or anywhere else has about the same amount of electronics as households in developed nations. We know this because of actual, measurable electricity consumption. The International Energy Agency says that per capita power consumption in the United States keeps increasing. In developing nations, it's increasing even faster because more people are consuming more power-hungry things. Most of the people on this planet live around the equator, where it's hot. Really hot. So when those folks get a little more cash in their jeans, they buy things like refrigerators and air-conditioning, two of the biggest users of electricity in any home. You've probably never given a second thought to the implications of air-conditioning, but let me tell you, that's a type of technology that is nearly as revolutionary as the automobile, if not more so. Every trend that has come to define modern life can eventually be traced back to the proliferation of air-conditioning."

"Right . . . Is this the part where you reveal yourself to be an air-conditioning salesman?"

"Doc, put your thinking cap back on. The United States uses as much electricity for air-conditioning, a 'want' not a 'need,' as the entire continent of Africa uses for everything. That's another little factoid for you. Imagine living in Nevada, Arizona, or New Mexico without air-conditioning—it simply would not sustain modern life. The fact that we now have tens of millions of people living in the Sun Belt is a direct by-product of air-conditioning. And hey, you're a doctor, so you should know that conception rates decline with rising temperatures, and that cooler temperatures increase the viability of sperm, right?"

"Well, I'd have to go back and check my textbooks," I smiled, "but yes, I believe that's right."

"What I'm getting at is that an invention like air-conditioning has a profound effect on human life, not just comfort, but everything. And the warmer the world gets, the more the world needs air-conditioning. If we can acknowledge how air-conditioners have impacted life in America, imagine how important it will be in China and India. You can bet your bottom dollar that if we think an air conditioner is a necessity, so will they!"

"Let's not forget about other conveniences, ones that emancipated so many women—the household washing machine, for example."

"Just imagine what it takes to achieve that seemingly simple task without a machine. We load it, press a button, and then get on with our productive day. What do all those women do without it?"

"I know it has been called one of the greatest inventions of the industrial revolution."

"For the billions still washing the 'old-fashioned' way, almost always the women of the family in the developing world, what do they do to achieve this simple yet vital task? They need to source the water, usually some distance away from their homes, heat it, and in the process waste half of their day to complete this otherwise basic task we are entitled to. This is the very definition of significant effort with near-zero productivity. Do you think they all want a washing machine?"

"Obviously. Why wouldn't they?"

"Without a doubt! And who are we to deny them that basic privilege and key to freedom? That brings me to part two of my eureka moment, the question of how we're going to power all these things that have a cord sticking out of the back of them."

"So now you're talking about electricity as in power?"

"Where does all of our electricity come from to supply all this technology and unstoppable growth? And where is it going to come from? Ever since the World's Fair in Paris, societies have consumed more and more energy. We purchase things that require electricity to function, forcing government and industry to generate more electricity and transfer that energy from where it is generated to the consumer. As demonstrated on that mountaintop, the wireless phenomenon has reached into every corner of the globe."

"More people consuming more things and that includes more electricity."

"You just knocked it out of the park, Doc. Home run. Now, let's round the bases. Energy means electricity and electricity needs one thing to make it possible. Guess what that is."

"Oil? Coal? Uranium? Natural gas? Any of those will work. I give up, what is the most important thing to make electricity?"

"Copper! The red metal is the common bond that is a constant no matter how you create electricity. Oil, coal, uranium, or natural gas are used to make energy and energy equals electricity, but electricity needs copper! Fossil fuels in automobiles can be substituted, of course. However, when that takes place, usually in the form of electric cars, we need to store energy. All these green cars need to be fueled on a daily basis, which requires electricity, and that needs copper too!"

"And you are an expert on copper because you were an electrician?"

"Who else could better understand this relationship? And the future? What does everyone talk about these days when it comes to making electricity?"

"Green energy, of course—solar power, wind power . . ."

"And none of it is possible without copper. It's the common bond, one hundred percent of the time. If I wanted to be fair to myself and fully explore the turning point in my life, it was when I wanted to know everything there was to know about the red metal. I became obsessed with every conceivable facet related to it. So that's how I won the lottery three times. First, because I started my career in the mid-nineties installing rapidly advancing technology on a massive scale. Second, I chose to become an electrician who understood the upstream and downstream significance of rapidly changing technology. And third, because I just happened to be doing it between Seattle, a technology capital of the world, and Vancouver, a commodity capital for those who find, produce, and provide the red metal to industry and consumers."

"That means that technology is directly connected to electricity which is directly connected to copper and commodities?"

"Doc, technology's been the red herring during this entire discussion. We can both accept that things are changing at lightning speed. The point I am now trying to underline for you goes back to my moment on the mountaintop, everything—and I mean absolutely everything—with respect to the technology up here comes from the commodities down there. Period. No matter what is invented. And there will be tons of new computers, applications, software, cloud networking, whatever. None of it is possible without copper and other commodities."

"More people consuming more things—in other words, *stuff* that has a power cord sticking out of the back of it—means more people consuming electricity, which means more people consuming copper."

"Yup, but just try to grasp the scope of it. Beyond the billions of gadgets that will fill the homes of those people making the great leap from rural to urban, even their homes will require that stuff down there. Let's take it back to Tianjin, a city of the future where they have transformed a toxic dump into a sustainable supercity. China and India and others in the developing world are going to be building megaprojects like this for some time, and these projects will be more reliant on electricity than ever, and they'll need copper and many other commodities to make it happen."

"So you are suggesting that I follow commodities as a financial soap opera?"

"Yes. That is one of the financial soap operas every investor must follow. The PhD of the economy is copper. That's why the red metal is often referred to as 'Doctor Copper.' But it's not just copper, there is a whole basket of commodities that you should be aware of—oil, iron ore, zinc, gold, silver, cotton, coffee, and the list goes on."

"I was thinking you were just trying to appeal to me, but come to think of it, I have heard the term 'Doctor Copper' on Bloomberg, I believe. But I never really paid attention to it. You say it has a PhD, but why? And in what?"

"In economics, Doc. Even before this surge I'm speaking of, copper was needed for pipes and wiring, so a society that was doing well and growing used more copper. Demand for copper tells us how healthy the economy is. And that's as true as ever, if not more so, with all our new *stuff*."

"Johnny, the reason I was never interested in commodities is because I always found them terribly boring. But now I can visualize how they shape our economy and impact our world. The reason you were stressing the ingredients in the Big Mac was to show the relevance of all the commodities that make it possible."

"Commodities, boring? Well, that depends how you follow them. You need to look deeper, see the bigger picture, and connect the dots. Commodities represent the evolution of civilization and the ascent of man. When you put them in the context of the overall economy, the colossal demographic shift that is taking place, and rapidly evolving technology, it's actually a thrilling subject, the Big Mac being just one way to put commodities into perspective. You asked me what kind of sectors and writers to subscribe to as you begin your financial soap operas. Your suggestion was biotechnology or life sciences, both being great choices. However, for a building block to sound investment acumen, I'll hook you up with the daily soap opera I follow every day. It's a well-written six or seven pages, delivered every morning before the market opens, that touches on politics, currencies, stock markets, commodities, and current events. Following this daily financial soap opera will give you the macro knowledge you'll need as you identify the actual sectors you are going to follow. We'll call this the foundation to your investment knowledge base. It's not cheap, but it is well worth it."

I prided myself on being a student of history, but I now felt I had overlooked a strong undercurrent that had been bubbling beneath us since the dawn of electricity. The world had changed, and technology never stops to catch its breath. From Edison's lightbulb to the specialized lighting in my kitchen and everything in between, there was one theme that tied it all together, and it was very heavy and deep underground.

I was already spending a couple hours a day reading my usual newspapers so I didn't see any reason to ignore Johnny's advice to start following this daily newsletter he recommended. If I was going to make a real effort to change my investing philosophy, I needed the best information available and it was going to cost more than peanuts. I was going to become a financial soap opera junkie, and it was going to start by accepting that Doctor Copper was the PhD of the economy and that everything from up here truly did come from down there.

The spending class

It had been just over a month since I first started meeting with Johnny and I was pleasantly surprised at how much it had already impacted my daily routine. Rather than wake up and flip on the white noise of rolling business news, I now awoke to a fresh daily newsletter in my inbox, updating the various subplots of our financial world and most of the current events going on. Given the price—and it was pricey—I was skeptical about subscribing to it at first, but in the first week alone it had provided more intel, and dare I say entertainment, than I would have received from anything in my prior routine.

The most important takeaway from our last two meetings was the fact that by 2050 there will be nine billion people sharing our planet's finite resources. For those who think falling birth rates will affect future population growth, there is the more immediate impact of the one billion or so existing human beings that were about to become consumers. If a youthful electrician on a mountaintop can have an epiphany that permanently changes the course of his life, then could a middle-aged doctor like me clue into the ramifications of the largest migration of human beings in the history of the world, and attempt to profit gloriously from it? It was worth a shot.

Another collateral benefit I was already realizing was my broader understanding of green energy. I'd ordered a set of solar panels to install on my rooftop that would go some way in powering my various appliances and home automation system. As a result, my dream of building my very own interpretation of a Frank Lloyd Wright classic with modern touches had become that much more real.

I had scheduled a day off and even though it was only 7 a.m., I had already devoured today's newsletter and was eagerly awaiting Johnny's arrival. He'd offered me a chance to take his Porsche out for a spin and told me to wear something comfortable in case we went for a walk. Just as I put on the windbreaker that I usually wore to golf, I heard two honks from his Teutonic devil and went outside to find him waiting with a surprisingly alert grin on his face.

"Mornin', Doc. We'll get our coffee at our first stop. It's never a good idea to place boiling hot liquids in front of your face while attempting turns that pull a G or two of force."

"Cute. A little spin doesn't mean a Formula 1 lap. Remember, Johnny, I've still got kids and a business that rely on me. You know, little things called responsibilities."

After I jumped in and buckled up, I was surprised how roomy and comfortable this modern sports car was. I remembered a friend in college who drove his father's earlier edition that was a far cry from the efficient monument of decadence we were about to test. As usual, Johnny got right into our topic du jour.

"We've covered a lot of material over the past couple meetings, so I thought it would be a great time to recap the main theme of demographics and more people consuming more things in a little more detail."

"The granddaddy of all migrations currently underway."

"Tens of millions of people entering the world of consumerism like you and me," he said, smoothly peeling back out my driveway and into the street.

"I'm still skeptical about that one, Johnny. No matter what they do, there is no way that they become middle class just by moving to an urban setting. Even you admit it takes decades for that to fully happen."

"Does it? And by 'middle class,' what do you mean, Doc?"

"Exactly what it says. It's self-explanatory. By the time these migrating hordes actually have the earning power of a true middle class, decades will pass by."

"First of all, you need to get that word out of your vocabulary. The more relevant term is 'spending class' and the real question you should be asking is—what is their economic footprint? You may be surprised."

"By 'spending class,' are you suggesting a new class somewhere between middle class and, pardon the expression, lower class?"

"Not at all. The spending class is the new wave of consumers. We already talked about the sheer numbers of people that have left poverty and will continue to do so. What I'm talking about now is when those folks become bona fide consumers or, as I say, a spending class. They are nowhere close to having the earning power of the average American, but they have a similar economic footprint. For example, when someone in Thailand drives a Toyota five hundred kilometers, (about three hundred miles) it takes the exact same amount of gasoline as someone in Ohio driving the same car."

"No kidding."

"And when they want air-conditioning and power windows, it takes the exact same amount of copper to run those conveniences whether the Toyota is built and purchased in Asia or the United States. That's what I mean when I say economic footprint."

"So an economic footprint means the fallout of when these spending-class folks—or anyone for that matter—buy anything? How big is this spending class?"

"First, you need to put it into a local perspective to give credence to an estimated number. For that, we can use your antiquated idea of a middle class as the multiplier. To illustrate, let's use the United States, which has a large population and the biggest per capita middle class in the world. How many people live in the United States?"

"Just over three hundred million."

"Exactly. I have found that the best way to measure the middle class, and by default the spending class, is by understanding automobile sales. Up until the 2008 financial crisis, the United States was the largest market for automobile sales, by far, of any country in the world. And that makes sense because it has the largest middle class. Agreed?"

"No argument here."

"Okay. Well, if that has been established, how many new cars were sold to sustain this large middle class on an annual basis? The answer is between fourteen and sixteen million, from the mid-nineties up until the 2008 economic crisis, which crushed new car sales for the obvious reason, lack of consumer confidence. It can then be considered with a high degree of confidence that it takes approximately fifteen million new car sales each year to sustain a middle-class population of approximately three hundred million. Cars do not last forever, as we know, so that is a reliable example to demonstrate the spending power of a middle class."

"I'll give you that, but do those per capita percentages work in other nations, developing ones?"

"And then some. But more importantly, they can offer clues as to how big the actual spending class, those with real spending power, is in any society. Remember those cars don't care how much income you have, but they do put down the same economic footprint every time they are purchased. I once asked a group of executives, most of whom were very bearish on China and the developing world, how large the middle class in China was. I couldn't use my term, the spending class, because that would have been a whole different discussion."

"And what was their answer? You've already given me the clues, so I know the right answer is probably a ratio used in the formula. Fifteen million cars sold annually sustains approximately a spending class population of three hundred million, right?"

"Very good. Now all you need to know is how many cars are sold in China each year and you'll have your rough answer. And remember that in 1979 when Deng Xiaoping took over the Chinese economy, there were sixty privately owned cars in the whole country."

"What were the typical answers from your executive friends?"

"I'll get to that, but we should underline this reality— we already know that China is the same size, geographically speaking, as the United States, right?"

"Yes, we covered that—around 9.6 million square kilometers."

"And you also know that China's GDP has grown almost ten percent on average since 1979?"

"We glossed over that. I know it's dropped in recent years, but it's still way higher than the United States and most of the developed world."

"If you saw a map of China, could you name or, even better, simply locate five different cities?"

"Not likely."

"Precisely. And most other passive investors are the same. They only see the headlines on page one and they rarely look at the fundamentals of more people consuming more things. By 2025, there will be 220 cities in China with more than a million people. So to answer your question, most of my executive friends got the answer totally wrong. The only ones who were even close had actually been to China. Their guesses on how many spending-class folks there were in China ranged between twenty million, forty million, and fifty million people with an economic footprint."

"Okay, professor, how big is China's spending class or middle class or whatever you want to call it according to your system?"

"China has surpassed twenty million automobile units sold each year and almost every major auto manufacturer counts the Chinese market as their largest. They surpassed the United States after the economic crisis and have never looked back. This would suggest that the spending class in China is over four hundred million people, and growing by the day. And who can argue with that? Think about the total lack of awareness in assuming that the spending class, or as some still call it middle class, is the same size as a country's one-year automobile sales!"

"Twenty million automobile sales in China? Every year? Really? And we only have fifteen million here in the US?"

"Think of the impact that has had on oil consumption and the impact it's going to continue to have. And the majority of the parabolic increase in sales has happened in the past ten years!"

"So the basis of following the buying patterns of this demographic bulge is because it's real, because they actually do buy *stuff*?"

"You got it. And it's not just cars. Anyone can agree that these folks may not make fifty thousand a year like so-called Western consumers, but that's not the point. What is their actual economic . . . ?"

Johnny paused and mouthed the end of his sentence, which, by now, I knew by heart.

"Economic footprint?"

"*Hallelujah!* Yes! I couldn't give a damn about how much money any one of those four hundred million spending-class folks earns per month or per year. What I do know is that they are buying twenty million cars per year. I also know that they are living more and more comfortable lifestyles. Textbook statistics and the nineteenth-century model of GDP and gross national income—GNI, as the experts say—do not tell the story of their true economic footprint. When someone in the developing world earns ten thousand a year, they're likely to spend every penny of that money on purchasing their first convenience products. And, of course, they all need electricity to operate."

"There's an electrical cord sticking out of the end of everything they're going to buy."

"Right. And the first things they are buying are symbols of basic wealth that increase their level of comfort."

"Air-conditioning, refrigerators, and other three-C items."

"Air-conditioning is a triple whammy for anyone's economic footprint. A typical split-system air-conditioning unit, the kind you see hanging from any apartment window around the world, contains ten to fifteen pounds of copper for the wiring and piping. These things are then wired to their homes and powered up—this is the second whammy because they become the largest draw of electricity in a typical household. Finally, the third whammy happens during the hottest days of the year, when everyone turns them on all at once. That may not matter to someone who doesn't follow financial soap operas, but those that do, we know that there have been massive blackouts because entire countries are deficient in power generation. Even a place like Russia, with an otherwise cold climate, is host to apartment blocks littered with millions of air-conditioning units hanging from every window. The whole electrical system needs to be upgraded in order to support it."

"Energy equals electricity and electricity needs copper, no matter how it's generated."

"Music, Doc, sweet music to my ears. You can't obtain this information from a newspaper because few, if any, would ever write about it. But the facts are the facts. And this is not going to stop. There are estimates that China's urban population could reach one billion between 2025 and 2030."

We continued to talk about what he had branded as the "spending class" as we cruised out of the city and into the wild green yonder. He drove north until we pulled off the interstate and headed west. I guessed that we were aiming for the seaside. Our discussion had centered on this new class of consumer whose economic footprint would not be too much different from the folks who lived in the neighborhoods we passed along the way. When someone in America or other developed nations earns the average GNI, most of that money is not saved. In fact, it is used on mortgages, rent, car payments, and the day-to-day costs of just getting by. Any working-class person in America knows that when they earn $40,000 or $50,000 per year, they are not wealthy. Their actual economic footprint has been static for decades. It made sense that someone whose income was far smaller, but rapidly expanding, would spend almost all of their money playing catch-up purchasing their first everything.

"So, Johnny, let me recap the spending class and the fuel of their increasing economic footprints. I can now see that people around the world are getting wealthier and healthier and it's not going to stop. I can also see that it's not necessarily total income as recorded by traditional statistics, but if we looked at these folks like they were businesses, it'd be more about free cash flow, right?" I asked.

"Dramatic salary escalation has been the source of noticeably increasing spending patterns and, in turn, economic footprints. I call it the Prague Syndrome, which pertains to rapid salary escalation. When the Czech Republic and Slovakia separated back in 1993, after the Velvet Revolution, both those countries were coming out of forty years of communism. They were not considered wealthy by any means and in fact you could have said they were downright destitute. What they did have, Prague in particular, was a medieval architecture-loving tourist's dream and so tourists from around the globe invaded the gothic wonderland to buy postcards and eat Bohemian dumplings. Businesses were popping up like mushrooms to feed the insatiable demand and employee turnover was rampant. Just as a new restaurant would open, its staff would be stolen due to higher wage offers, forcing existing owners to match or beat the new standards. The real earning power of the average Eastern European has increased four or fivefold in the decades after the Cold War ended. This obviously has not been the case in the United States or Western Europe, has it?"

"Not even close. I don't think anyone I know could boast of even a fifty percent wage increase over the past twenty years."

"So, if your salary doubled every three or four years, you'd have lots of consumer confidence too, wouldn't you?"

"Who wouldn't!"

"The hyperinflation that plagued the world thirty years ago is gone—not one country suffers from it anymore, Zimbabwe being the last until they dollarized their economy."

"And what does that have to do with the spending class and economic footprints?"

"Recessions rob citizens of what they might have, whereas hyperinflation robs you of what you already have. In 1979, there were over thirty developing countries suffering from hyperinflation. Today, there are zero. What does that newfound confidence do to the emerging classes?"

"Unleashes a tremendous amount of newfound confidence and optimism, obviously."

"All over the world, this new spending class has found wealth, anchored by this confidence and optimism we haven't experienced in two generations. And they are buying *stuff* on a scale never seen in history."

"And all of it needs power."

"Same as here, same as Europe. They want the same things we have. And let me tell you, none of their children are playing with hula hoops or spinning tops."

As he finished that thought, we pulled into a large parking lot overlooking a vast industrial complex. I'd seen this sprawling complex before but had never taken the time to absorb the scale of it. It was clear that this was our destination all along when we stopped dead-center in front of the main structure.

"What do you see?" Johnny asked me.

"That's the largest industrial factory I've ever seen in my life."

"No matter if you're rich or poor, upper class or lower class, whether you live in Mumbai or New York, you cannot live without it. That, Doctor Anderson, is an oil refinery."

"Even if you're a hermit and live in a solar-powered organic oasis?"

"Even then. Oil refineries not only make gasoline, heating fuel, and lubricants possible, they also provide specialized fuels like distillates and kerosene for the jet aircraft we fly in. This kind of infrastructure is vital for any growing society. Even if you want to drive your brand-new electric car, it requires rubber tires and you still need to charge it. And that requires electricity."

"So no matter what kind of transportation we use, we still need refineries. And when it comes to creating electricity, the greener and cleaner it's generated, the more that's demanded of copper."

"That's right, Doc. I am an environmentalist. But I know the world is not going to stop advancing. Greens can choose whatever method of making electricity they see fit because I know green energy translates into more demand for copper. Even their electric cars need three to four times more copper per vehicle than a gasoline engine—and they still need to be charged. Simply put, traditional methods of making energy need lots of copper, but greener methods need even more. Do you know what a NIMBY is Doc?"

"Some kind of a hotdog?"

"Let me spell it out for you: N-I-M-B-Y—and it stands for Not-In-My-Back-Yard. That's what they might as well call that refinery. Nobody wants a new refinery to be built, or a new copper mine, or an oil pipeline, or anything that even comes close. Could you imagine how hard it would be to build that refinery today?"

"Damn near impossible."

"Without a doubt. So, can you not see the value in the ones that are already there?"

"Let me guess. You're also an expert on refineries and pipelines?"

"I follow energy. Energy, in all its forms, is one of my economic soap operas. We all need it and no one can live without it. Industry can shift between fuel sources, bouncing from coal to nuclear or oil to natural gas, and we are slowly but surely transitioning to more and more renewables. But make no mistake, the common bond is always copper, no matter which energy source is used."

"The umbilical cord of human progress—energy equals electricity."

"The lesson to be learned from visiting a site like this is: How will the nine billion people in 2050 have the things you and I take for granted? Does it not make sense to know and understand the policies that affect them and the patterns that make them relevant?"

"I'm ready to pinpoint my second financial soap opera, Johnny. Perhaps it's time we attended one of these conferences you talk so highly of?"

"My thoughts exactly. The New Orleans event, my top destination of the year if you recall, will take place one month from now. I'm already booked. I suggest you buy your plane ticket today."

Johnny had used a tip from an über-successful individual to become a participant in a whole new way of following financial markets. For him, that journey came full circle at get-togethers surrounded by contrarians where he was able to use his outlier expertise to offer insights into the backbone of global growth—energy. My advantage was my accelerated introduction provided by this storytelling electrician. Converting everything I was learning into action required that I attend the Mecca of alternative thinking.

The 4% club

The New Orleans Contrarian Investing Conference was fast approaching and I found myself spending all my free time researching the finer details of attending. As I was investing over $3,000 to cover my travel costs, accommodation, and admission, not to mention the five days and nights out of my valuable schedule, it was the prudent thing to do.

Aside from getting the most bang for my buck, I wanted to be prepared. I was about to take a meaningful and pricey departure away from the investment philosophy I had stuck with for most of my life, so not only did I want to know everything there was to know about what I was getting into, but I wanted to be able to capitalize efficiently on my time spent at the conference. If I was going to be a participant, I needed to participate.

There would be over five hundred different companies showcasing their assets and as many senior executives to talk to, so I even went so far as to research these. Over and above the myriad of investment opportunities, there would be dozens of well-respected newsletter writers to listen to and a keynote debate featuring a Republican, a Democrat, and a revered Libertarian. I could hardly wait.

The flight from Seattle to New Orleans was around six hours, providing me with enough time for one last skim over everything I'd learned in the past months. We had covered the demographics of population growth, more people consuming more things, and how technology would affect and be affected by it all.

While it was true that it was difficult to predict the short-term effects of government policy and economic earthquakes, especially in a post-crisis world, this unstoppable army of new consumers would be our focus when we touched down in New Orleans. I was going to apply these months of hard work to try to find the proverbial needle in a haystack. I had found my first major theme in population growth, but I wanted to secure something else to follow closely, meet a mentor to help guide me with updates in the future, and hopefully land some contrarian investments. And if all else failed, Johnny had attended this conference many times, so he was my trump card.

When we rolled out of Louis Armstrong International to hail a cab, the first thing to hit me was the heat. It was hot but not too humid, a welcome departure from the relentless downpour that had overtaken Washington state since the first leaves had begun to fall.

"Your first time to the Big Easy?" Johnny asked when I stopped for a minute to take off my jacket. "I told you that you wouldn't need that jacket."

"It's fantastic. I'm finally crossing it off the bucket list I never knew I had."

"This is my favorite city in the world and you're about to see why. We're staying in the hotel attached to the show.

I always do. Not only does it save time, all the major CEOs and speakers are there too. It's twice as expensive when you book late but invaluable if you meet someone in the elevator, or better yet, swing an off-the-cuff breakfast or lunch together."

Johnny's saying—"if you pay peanuts, you get monkeys"—began to ring truer and truer. Aside from investing, it seemed to work in many other aspects of life. I reflected back on all the crappy sunglasses or shoes I'd purchased over the years just to watch them fall apart or break. Buy high-quality once, or buy garbage thrice; either way you're paying the same, but when you pay peanuts, you're stuck with mediocrity.

I was especially impressed in respect to his choosing a more expensive, yet highly strategically located hotel, which is something I never would have considered on my own. I could have saved money on the room and opted for the Best Western, but I'd only be getting half of the experience and even less of the access. There was a sweet sense of satisfaction knowing that I was getting a bargain by paying twice as much as other attendees for this distinct advantage.

"I'm just glad they had space," I told Johnny as our cab pulled up to the hotel, our baggage swiftly picked up by a duo of discreet bellhops.

"The hotel is booked a year in advance for events like these, mostly for the VIPs, but they always leave a few rooms, at double the price, for last-minute reservations or guys like you and me who insist on being here. They know that and they know that twice the price is still a bargain for what we'll be getting."

"All right, Johnny, we're going to make the best of it and I've mapped out each day's highlights, so why don't we . . ."

"Whoa there, Doc. You're getting a little bit ahead of yourself. Let's start by figuring out who we *aren't* going to spend any time with."

"I was thinking we were here to meet everyone and see everything."

"The conference lasts four days. There are five hundred companies and thirty presentations per day, panels and keynotes, plus the social events."

"Exactly. So I thought I could go through the aisles and cover a hundred and fifty companies per day, in between sitting in on fifteen stage presentations. And naturally, the keynotes are a given."

"So you want to find out everything you can about investing in assisted living partnerships? How about commercial real estate opportunities? There's also an interesting discussion on shifting tides in mutual-fund performance fees to which you probably want to dedicate an entire two hours."

"You've made your point. I spent weeks preparing, so I do have a shortlist and I don't want to address anything that is not connected to, as you put it, the largest migration of human beings in history. I was simply thinking that I could scan the showroom floor to get a feel for how it works."

"I did the same my first time through, and there's value in that approach, sure. But when you have the advantage of accelerating your familiarity with knowing who's who in the zoo, it's far better than throwing darts at the showroom floor. Even if you didn't have me as a guide, any new investor's early foray into contrarian investing should be focused on finding out what they want to invest in. You already know that the theme is population growth and how it affects energy, consumption, commodities, and Doctor Copper. Now, you need to know who the perennial winners are. I personally take a more strategic approach, starting with a qualified shortlist and then spending my limited event time being surrounded by them. But I always start with my 4% Club."

"Your 4% Club? You brought that up before. Fill me in on the meaning of that."

"The 4% Club comes from Pareto's Law. That was coined by the Italian economist of the same name who discovered a principle that twenty percent of the effort creates eighty percent of the gain. It was later observed that this worked in many facets of the economy and in society. It was also seen that the twenty percent on the other end of the spectrum causes eighty percent of the problems and misery. Over one hundred years later, it's still relevant and we can see numerous examples including our urban-to-rural migration example."

"So that's the 80/20 rule. I *have* heard about that, but how do you get down to four percent?"

"The 4% Club members are the top performers with respect to investing. Within Pareto's Law, there is yet another Pareto's Law. This would suggest that twenty percent of those original twenty percent, which is where the four percent comes from, create the overwhelming bulk of the super successes. This is especially true in regards to higher-risk contrarian investing."

"And on the other end of the spectrum? There are a few bad apples that create a disproportionate amount of the grief?"

"Sadly, that's the case. George Bernard Shaw expressed that exact sentiment when he said that 'horse racing is nothing more than a plot between the upper classes and the lower classes to fleece the middle classes.' This can easily be used to describe junior stock markets and speculative investments, or what you and I call contrarian investing."

"So those are the guys to steer clear of? And as it's hard to tell who they are, you stay on the top part of Pareto's Law and only focus on those with an exceptional track record, which is the 4% Club?"

"If I can avoid it, I never approach a goat from the front, a horse from the back, or a fool from any side. Investing with fools is gambling whereas investing with those that have had four or five or more positive outcomes for shareholders is confident, intelligent investing. And if I can buy those management teams at a discount, when markets correct, then that is the true definition of contrarian investing."

"What are some of the factors that differentiate a four-percenter from others?"

"The four-percenters that I follow always have the most skin in the game. That means the investor that has the most to lose is the four-percenter. There are too many company executives who are working more for salary and stock options and less for stakeholder appreciation. You and I, as investors, only make money one way: when the shares we buy and hold appreciate. Some of the four-percenters I follow don't even take a salary! They make money when the investor makes money, a true alignment with the investor's interest. If things don't work out, they will be the single biggest losers. Just the same, when things work out, they stand to make the most profit—which, by the way, has historically happened more often and totally out of proportion to the industry average."

"So, for these reasons, you want us to spend all of our time following the 4% Club?"

"If you don't allocate your time to a condensed format within the overall conference, then after four days you'll find yourself confused and conflicted and you'll end up with too much unusable information. Besides, the conference is only eight hours a day and you want to sit in on at least fifteen talks during those eight hours. After all, that's why we're here. But that would leave you with only a couple minutes per company."

"In other words, running around like a chicken with no head on is not a strategy."

"What you're forgetting is the advice that the tycoon gave me and I gave you. There are teams of famous newsletter analysts that comb the conference floor for you. They already know all the players in the sectors they follow, so you don't have to waste your time researching total strangers. You can accelerate your education by listening to your shortlist of favorite writers, follow their filtered list, and then concentrate on the overlap that occurs when you see our four-percenters involved with those picks. That's when all the planets align and you can invest with more confidence. That's exactly what that tycoon did, it's what I do, and it's worked for both of us."

"You're right again. If I'm going to pay someone for great ideas and information, they can do the walking for me. When I narrow it down, due to my reading and research, I can then zero in on specific companies and request discussions with their executives. So I should spend my time listening to and interviewing the newsletter writers of interest who have expertise in my favorite fields of consumption, commodities, and copper?"

"Doc, who's teaching you? Buy that man a cape!"

It was only day one and that meant the lightest schedule of the conference and time for attendees to enjoy a kick-off cocktail. Rather than gather before the main event, I wanted to go back to my room and adjust my attack list. What was clear is that we were going to focus on the analysts that cover the companies that offered the best opportunity to feed the spending class.

Johnny, on the other hand, wanted to rub elbows with the many friends and contacts he had met over the years. I needed to reassess, and wasn't quite ready to dive headfirst into the swimming pool, so I went to relax in my room, enjoy a bourbon—if you're in the South, might as well drink what the locals drink—and pour over the conference literature.

Understanding who I wanted to listen to was important because they were the ones I wanted to meet. Were the other attendees going to be as focused as Johnny and I were?

With so many valid opportunities readily available, how many of my fellow contrarians were going to be fixated on the theme of consumption in the developing world? One thing was for sure, I was going to have a razor-sharp focus and not let anything stand in the way of yours truly having pure and unfettered access to the experts of my new-found passion.

The keynote

If you don't travel that often, like me, then you cannot truly appreciate the gravity of the term jet lag as you've probably become conditioned to hearing it. In the medical field, we call it "desynchronosis," the Latin for "unsynchronized," as transmeridian air travel tends to rapidly alter your circadian rhythm, resulting in sleep disruption, decreased cognitive ability, headaches, irritability, and sometimes indigestion. Basically, it takes a hammer to your internal clock if not managed properly.

There was just a two-hour time difference between the West Coast and the Big Easy, but the loss of those precious few hours had already taken its toll on me. As soon as I woke up, I felt the need to supplement my typical two cups of morning coffee with an extra shot of espresso, a room service splurge which left me jittery and anxious on a day where I was already both of those things. By the time I came to my senses, I realized it was nearly time to hit the conference floor and I was furiously reviewing my notes like I was back in university cramming for an exam. To say I was excited was an understatement. I was giddier than a schoolgirl on Valentine's Day.

The only professional gatherings I usually attended were the humdrum annual Medical Association meetings. Listening to my colleagues pontificate on the effects of this new drug or that old treatment was about as exciting as listening to someone describe the science behind solving a Rubik's Cube. The world of contrarian investing was an entirely different beast—it was an art, not a science.

Being located at the event hotel provided a convenient home base from which to operate and enabled Johnny and me quick in-and-out access to everything we wanted to attend. Our first breakfast was served as the start of the conference and took place in an open and social atmosphere. The most unique aspect of this walk-and-talk format was the vast amount of hand-selected companies and executives from totally diverse fields: biotechnology, natural resource companies, metals and energy, high tech, and real estate income funds. There was even a group from Argentina selling a "lifestyle" community put forward as the real-life version of "Galt's Gulch" from *Atlas Shrugged*.

Intermingling with this eclectic group were curious participants like myself, authors of well-known books, newsletter writers from the conference agenda, various high-profile investors, and even some notable politicians. This was a genuine potpourri of economic intelligence and investment firepower—it felt like you couldn't brush the opportunity away if you tried, and I was standing there smack-dab in the middle just trying to absorb it all.

A few faces recurred in the mix, seemingly always knowing where they were headed and with anyone they stopped to talk to greeting them like an old friend. They were all sharply dressed and must have had special maps which let them pop in and out of secret passages—I'd see one on one side of the room, then suddenly on the other, while I'd barely made any progress. Most notable among these was a striking Indian woman, maybe a bit younger than me, wearing what seemed to fall halfway between a traditional sari and high-end Parisian fashion. I tried not to let the sight of her pull my eyes away from whomever I was talking to whenever I caught a glimpse of her, but usually without success.

After I had milled around for about ten minutes, trying not to be bewildered or at least not to look it, someone tapped my shoulder. I looked around and saw no one there, only to turn back and find Johnny at my side.

"I can't believe you fell for that old gag, Doc!"

As I turned around to face Johnny, I saw a small crowd gather around a distant figure. Like a moth to a warm light, I was also curious about what was going on and so had been gravitating toward the gawkers.

"Who's that?"

"The keynote speaker."

"But it's only breakfast time."

"Every day, there's a kick-off speaker, a lunch speaker, and a final panel, over and above the daily agenda. However, the first talk of the conference is always something to look forward to. And this year, we're in for a real treat."

"Wow. When I was reviewing the agenda last night, it listed the first speaker as a mining executive; not exactly what I would call speaker-hall fireworks."

"Once you've heard all the talks, met with most of the newsletter crowd, and glad-handed with your fellow contrarians, you can tell me who you thought was the most engaging. For now, I can only tell you that he's well worth the billing as the conference inaugurator."

The crowd continued to build around this mining maven. His biography stated that he had successfully sold three companies for billions and was always the single largest shareholder in each instance. That would suggest he was a legitimate tycoon, but it did not explain why the conference organizers would choose some rock jockey over a high-flying tech geek or real estate mogul to open things up. There would seem to be more to anticipate from a former politician or wordsmith than what I could hope for from someone who dug up rocks for a living.

"Well, he sure has a following. That's a huge crowd over there."

"What have we been talking about for the past couple of months? More people consuming more things. It's time we start putting this information together thoughtfully, since it weaves the relevance and importance of that macro theme into opportunities."

"My pencil is sharp and notepad open. All we need now is a fresh cup of coffee and front-row-center seats."

We worked our way into the presentation hall and, even though we were ten minutes ahead of the scheduled conference introduction, there was barely a seat to be had.

"Holy smokes! This place is packed."

"If you want really good seats, you must get here early."

We found ourselves a decent vantage point, one of the large projection screens centered in front of us. The conference organizer, a well-known writer and newsletter publisher, outlined the focus and theme for the next three days, "Global Growth, Yes or No?," then gave a colorful introduction to the mining tycoon that detailed his background and experience.

While listening to the introduction and the guy's rather dynamite CV, I thought to myself that some forward-thinking TV network should produce a reality show about him. His life was so wild, I was getting dizzy just listening about it. I realized just how much I must have glossed over his biography in the conference agenda. In the course of a week, he could be working on Wall Street, then take a break to fly deep into the jungles of Africa, then take off to a movie premiere in Paris, in between which he would find time to share a scotch with any number of world leaders, all from the comfort of his own private jet.

Before I heard him speak one word, I had been captivated by the introduction afforded him, which likened him to one of the iconoclasts who would be hanging out in the Argentine Galt's Gulch. The most incredible part of his legend was the unreal fact that the salary he took to run his entire empire was just one dollar per year. He only made money when his stakeholders made money. He was beyond a fourpercenter; he was Rockefeller, Steve Jobs, and Teddy Roosevelt all wrapped up in one, and it was immediately clear I wanted to follow his economic soap opera.

The question on every investor's mind sitting before him was "When will things be back to business as usual?" In the years following the 2008 economic collapse, various economies had fluttered between marginal growth and a new word entered the American lexicon that was old hat in the land of the rising sun—stagflation.

It was on everyone's lips, but nobody could answer that question nor could we expect our globe-trotting mining executive to answer it for us. What we did receive was a tour de force on the nature of our changing world that began with a very memorable figure of speech.

"Before I begin, I want you all to close your eyes and imagine you are a passenger riding on a train, rolling across the landscape. As a participant on this journey, you have two choices: to sit facing the oncoming scenery or to place yourself on the flipside, looking back on all that has passed. I'll give you a moment to decide."

Being a student of history, I chose to look back, and the landscape I imagined was much like the drive I took with Johnny through the Washington countryside. Skyscrapers blended into suburban communities, condos into factories, the oil refinery rushed past, and then came waves of evergreen trees and farmland.

"Investors with inadequate knowledge of history are frequently the most bearish. Let us use the past as a beacon to the future so we can all be a little less biased in a world filled with so much negativity. If you've chosen to sit looking forward, you are able to see what may come ahead but you may have already forgotten how we arrived here. For those that chose the back-facing view, you will be more prepared to build a comprehensive understanding of the future as you observe the changing landscape that forms the coming mountains and valleys. Both are good choices. However, for these uncertain times we want to look to the past to offer us clues as to what may happen as we forge ahead as a society."

It was a simply brilliant way to capture the attention and imagination of the listener, and it was the perfect set-up for the gist of his presentation. To my delight, he continued with a series of historical examples to build up to his more important points about investing.

He noted there had only been two major changes in the number one spot in global economic rankings since the industrial revolution began. Britain, protected by the world's largest navy at the time and fueled by world-leading reserves of coal and, in turn, steel production, would overtake China and India at the onset of her industrial revolution.

In the fifty years following the American Civil War, the United States would overtake Britain as the world's largest economy and has held that position ever since. As he reached his major point, he stated that it would only be a matter of time until China, with the world's largest population, would reclaim the title she had held for almost two thousand years.

"What is surprising most of the well-respected prognosticators at this time," he said, "is the acceleration of when China should be surpassing the United States as the world's largest economy."

He went on to describe that in 1992, the gross domestic product of the United States was over $6 trillion while in China it was under $500 billion. Twenty years later, the two countries' GDPs had climbed to over $15 trillion and $10 trillion respectively. Who's catching up to whom? In 1979, the average American was twenty times richer than the average Chinese citizen; now, we were less than five times richer and falling; a story told by every economic gap that has closed these past decades.

He noted that one billion people in China still do not live like you and me. The first thing that came to my mind was Johnny's catchphrase about how no army, no government, and no spiritual force could prevent that other one billion from participating in basic progress.

"If you haven't been there, like many of the Sino-bears living out there in the financial permafrost, then how can you know?"

It was true that many of the nattering naysayers had not been around the world. It had always been something that irked me. I'd rather draw my opinions from facts than assumptions.

"From up there, one can see what is down here," was a line that he clearly wanted to plant in everyone's mind as an image of hot air balloons floating over green fields filled the projection screen. He reiterated the fact that some of the deepest negativity, with respect to Asia and the growth bubbles people talked about, came from people who had never been there.

"I have been visiting Asia for thirty years and I have seen firsthand the explosive growth. It is not that the American experience is over, far from it, but what is happening is the penthouse of power and influence around the world is getting bigger."

The idea of cultural differences was reinforced with the insight that we in the West renovate whereas those in the East build anew. This was further established by highlighting the positive outlook that billions of people around the world still had. These folks were speculators in a more prosperous future and a speculator, by definition, was an optimist and not a pessimist like so many beaten-down citizens in the West. I had to ask myself, where was global growth going to come from? The US and Europe? Or from the hundreds of millions of emerging consumers?

"The biggest difference between the developed West and the emerging East is that when you multiply any number, no matter how small, by 2.5 billion, it becomes a very large number. In the West, we used to have the capital and the know-how. Now, they have the capital, and they already know how. When it comes to leadership between the two, there is a profound difference because most of the top political posts in China are held by people from the STEM fields. The members of the audience looking forward on our imaginary train probably forget what that stands for," he said with a cheeky grin and a light laugh, pointing at shadow figures.

"Let me refresh you—Science, Technology, Engineering, and Math—the STEM fields are the very foundations of any nation's brainpower. What is the typical professional background of the average American politician? Lawyer. Imagine, the vast majority of our elected decision-makers learn how to argue for a living. Is it any wonder little gets done in Congress, while the leaders of emerging economies learn how to build things?"

It was such a simple statement, yet the sobering reality of our country being led by lawyers gives one pause to think. In high school debate class, the training ground for many lawyers, you are taught to argue both sides of a topic. When you have debated the topic to exhaustion, your instructors might flip your point of view and make you argue the other side of that position. These professional arguers are the people who are guiding our nation forward. If it wasn't so sad, it might actually be funny.

"When it comes to public policy debates and infrastructure projects, we have limited representation by people who know how to make things. In China, they put their best and brightest at the helm, and it shows with their world-leading engineering and infrastructure projects."

He elaborated on real GDP and the reliability of reported statistics. He noted the Chinese leadership has three key metrics they use to follow the strength of their economy—rail freight traffic, electricity consumption, and debt and loan levels.

"Are these not the pulse of the health of any economy?" he asked.

"Where do you think the innovations of the future will come from?" he continued. "The choices made at the leadership level in any economy reverberate through the entire populace. In Western Europe, it is easier to divorce your wife than it is to fire an employee. Where can there be greater innovation or optimism? In that atmosphere of seniority and entitlement or in a place with far less business bureaucracy?"

It was true, in the West, one could obtain a divorce far easier than it was to improve productivity in big industry. But this may be changing as hard-working young people around the world prefer the opportunity of a career to the stifling effects of impossible hiring conditions.

"A final thought about cultural differences is that the majority of products purchased in China are paid for in cash. These folks are not carrying monstrous amounts of credit-card debt. Nor did they likely know, or care, that Lehman Brothers collapsed during the economic crisis. Little has been able to derail the individual ambitions of these industrious new consumers."

We learned about the BRIC (Brazil, Russia, India, China) countries, and more specifically CHINDIA (China, India), with other examples of how cultural stereotypes were being torn down. India, a country with thousands of elaborately stratified social and hereditary hierarchies, is well known for its caste system. Now, in the new global economy, a young entrepreneur in the lowest caste can be the wealthiest guy in the village. I thought to myself what that would do to unleash human potential in the country with the second-largest population in the world and a middle class larger than the entire United States.

"Since the financial economic crisis in 2008, there have been recessions all over the planet. Have there been many depressions? Has hyperinflation become rampant?"

He reiterated what Johnny had said about the differences between recessions and hyperinflation. Now I knew where Johnny had picked up the jewel of information.

"It is imperative that every investor in this room understand that recessions rob people of what they might have as businesses and governments curtail spending, leading to an unknown future, but this does pass. Hyperinflation, on the other hand, robs people of what they already have. Thank goodness it has been eradicated from the developing world, affording so many billions the confidence to strive for so much more."

There was a simple common-sense factor to those two scenarios. A recession was a condition that we in the United

States had faced many times in my lifetime. They were always terrible for the economy, and almost every time, they weighed heavily on my friends and family. But recessions do pass and confidence is rebuilt.

Hyperinflation was something that most people my age, particularly in the West, have never experienced. We have forgotten what that word really means and he reminded us all. When people are no longer concerned about losing what they already have, it surely unleashes the maximum in human potential. Hundreds of millions of people in countries around the world can celebrate that as they too are not worried about the albatross of hyperinflation.

His presentation shifted gears into a series of stories supported by useful facts. He would coin a term and then spin a yarn that would go around the world and come back to end with everyone in the audience feeling like a sudden expert on that brand-new term. One of these terms that would become the core statement of the entire trip was "Airpocalypse."

The developing world was becoming measurably wealthier, and that was a good thing. But its problem, and every human being's concern and opportunity, was an unprecedented level of smog choking the large cities of the Tiger economies. In the past, the citizenry would be left to suffer, but the time had come to finally deal with the environmental side effects of over thirty years of near ten percent year-over-year growth.

China now had three hundred million people with driver's licenses and, as I had learned from Johnny's lessons, it was and will remain the largest automobile market in the world. Over twenty million new cars were sold in China every year, and one of the unfortunate by-products of this stunning development was prolonged and heavy bouts of air pollution that plagued the citizens of her megacities. Asking these people to ditch their newly purchased cars and walk to work was not realistic, but what would help this growing crisis was making their emissions cleaner. And therein lay a very big opportunity that our keynoter was happy to explain to us as he went on to solve the concern and opportunity question.

"The way science makes gasoline and diesel engines cleaner is by capturing some of the tailpipe pollutants in a wondrous invention we call the catalytic converter. Palladium must be used for gasoline engines and platinum makes a diesel engine less polluting, and these are things anyone for cleaner air can applaud. Electric cars, which create zero emissions, need to be manufactured, fed, and properly nourished. All three of these processes demand copper, way more copper. Hydrogen fuel cells, being embraced all over the world, need *ounces* of platinum, not tenths of ounces! Ladies and gentlemen, copper, palladium, and platinum are your family of green metals so, if you are environmentally aware, you'll want to become more familiar with them because they are the only things that help clean up the Airpocalypse."

This point struck an interesting chord for me. I'd always been a huge booster for the environment and alternative energy, but never really acted on it. And I had definitely never drawn any parallel between the *stuff* down there and valuable green innovation up here. But why wasn't every investor piling into the inevitable theme of cleaner air in the developing world?

"How do they make electricity in China?" he questioned the crowd. "Coal, dirty brown coal, but that can't keep going on forever. Since Fukushima, Japan has turned off its nuclear reactors, so now how do they produce electricity? Coal and natural gas. Germany? They are having one of the biggest green energy renaissances and copper thanks them for it. But for now, their baseload power comes from guess what? Dirty brown coal. But the real question is how will they make electricity in the future? Green energy, or any form of energy for that matter, requires one thing every time—copper."

He implored the crowd to never forget one fact that was undeniable no matter how many negative headlines they saw: power consumption has never done anything but go up, and power needs copper. I'd heard it before from Johnny and now again from this experienced investor. This fact had now become biblical in nature.

"The Airpocalypse taking place in China's hundreds of cities, and all over the world, can only be cleaned up using more palladium, platinum, and copper. And there's only one way they are able to secure it—by importing it from people like me who actually own it."

The most shocking new development he outlined was that copper's usefulness could potentially expand beyond many of today's standard applications. Hospitals had started using copper for countertops, door handles, and other surfaces where bacteria were a problem.

"God forbid you should have to visit a hospital, but if you do, please be aware of your surroundings. You are going to see more and more copper, the most natural surface to repel bacteria. Stainless steel is a magnet for the nasties that make people sicker when they leave the hospital than when they arrived."

He finished this thought by urging everyone to do their own research on the historic relevance of copper in the medical field. It had been a known antibody for keeping sickness at bay for millennia. These implications for copper were mind-blowing over and above all the other uses. As a doctor, I knew he was right—it was becoming more prevalent and when one multiplied the number of medical clinics across only the United States, the implications for the copper industry were staggering.

"But things are serious and we continue to live in nervous times. *Nervous times.* If you invested in global growth ten years ago, should you abandon that philosophy lock, stock, and barrel due to potential stagflation in Europe and the West? Will the folks I just talked about stop being optimistic? Stop growing? Stop consuming? Will the ghost cities you read about derail the migration of one billion people? Have governments in established economies done anything to repair their pathetic balance sheets? You all know the obvious answers to these simple but important questions. Trillions of dollars have been printed and fed like drugs to greedy bankers while they secretly destroy your real spending power. How does one protect oneself? Own hard assets to retain real spending power! In China, and other parts of the world, copper is money, real money. Gold is money." His voice then dropped to a whisper and the silence throughout the room made it clear that everyone was hanging on every word. "Hard assets are money—they protect everyone's real spending power."

The allocated hour had passed so smoothly, it was as if he had been telling one continuous story and nobody wanted it to end. It was a full hour of current events, an encyclopedia of data points, and at least a half dozen unforgettable parables that everyone in attendance would recount for years to come.

All the while, this man who had made three fortunes in the world of mining only needed to whisper one sentence in support of his own prolific "green metal" deposits. The world could not live without his "green metals" and when they needed them, they would have to buy them from people like him. All he had to do was wait. I now had a thirst that needed to be quenched, and that thirst aligned with the actual business and passion of this geology promoter. A four-percenter who had shot way ahead to the front of the line of those I wanted to follow as my main economic soap opera.

"There has been lots of talk about 'the one percent,' and everyone here can recall the backlash to the fat cats on, Wall Street. Let me tell you, that is not the real one percent. Everyone here who is investing their valuable time and resources is in the *true* one percent, and here's why. Ask any ten people outside of this very exclusive gathering these simple questions and I guarantee you nine out of ten will get the answers wrong. In what measure do we value gold, iron ore, copper, wheat, and beef? And what is their current value? Knowing the answers to those questions, ladies and gentlemen, is your overwhelming advantage over ninety-nine percent of the population; thus you are all in the real one percent."

The clever way he ended his talk reminded me of something Johnny said during our first meeting at my house. Whereas Johnny had used the example of a Big Mac, it now made far more sense to me knowing how much the *stuff* that made a Big Mac possible actually cost. If a Big Mac was indexed to real inflation, then it made absolutely no sense that government CPI, consumer price index, excluded fuel and food.

Truth be told, before I met Johnny I'd have had no idea how much any of the building blocks to an economy were priced, let alone cost. There was great satisfaction knowing I too was in the one percent.

Lunch with the
realistic environmentalist

"If I hadn't been reading that newsletter you recommended, I would have failed that quiz across the board," I said to Johnny as we walked out of the presentation hall.

"You get the point, then?"

"Gold in ounces, copper in pounds, oil by the barrel, wheat in a bushel, and cattle by the head."

"And more importantly, you stay current on the prices so, like in a soap opera, you can follow the daily, monthly, and yearly swings and you know how much all that *stuff* actually costs."

As we filed onto the showroom floor, Johnny guided me toward the exit door, away from the maze of investment opportunities exhibits.

"Where are we going?" I asked.

"To meet a friend, someone who I think can really explain the relevance of where all this stuff comes from."

The hotel lobby was as busy as the conference itself, and hidden away in the bustle of it all was none other than our billionaire mining tycoon chatting away with someone. Johnny motioned me to follow and made a beeline for him. What was Johnny doing? Can we just go up to this guy and ask him questions?

I stopped wondering as we closed in and I realized who the tycoon was talking to—it was the striking Indian woman I'd seen earlier. There seemed to be an easy rapport between them as they both smiled and laughed but still maintained a presence that set them apart from the rest of the crowd.

To my surprise, the tycoon's face lit up as soon as he saw Johnny, as he reached out and clasped the younger man by the shoulder.

"It's been a while, Sparky."

"A year to the minute."

I was dumbfounded at the way in which Johnny was so cordially greeted by this man who had just received a standing ovation from a roomful of sophisticated investors. Even more impressive was that it seemed quite clear that the meeting we were about to have had been planned well in advance. The tycoon turned to the Indian woman, motioning to Johnny.

"Noorita, this is Johnny, an old friend. I call him 'Sparky.' He's almost as tenacious as you."

"Charmed," Noorita smiled, tilting her head slightly.

"Ms. Nair is in from Mumbai," the tycoon explained. "She's big in tech and communications."

"Great to meet you," Johnny replied warmly, bowing his head slightly.

"Who's your friend, another convert?" the tycoon asked, extending his hand for a firm handshake.

"Doc Anderson, my family doctor. He's taken it upon himself to broaden his horizons about the world we live in."

"Your speech certainly helped," I gushed as I shook his hand. "Ms. Nair, a pleasure to meet you."

I copied Johnny's head bow, unsure if it was the proper custom or if he possibly was faking it.

"Likewise, I'm sure, Doctor Anderson."

As she did for Johnny, she tilted her head and smiled again, though I was unsure if, this time, it was tinged with amusement at my gesture.

"Welcome aboard, Doc," the tycoon offered. "Were you able to pass my quiz at the end?"

"The answers were easy now that I follow these kinds of things, but as Sparky here would tell you, I'm still working on the broader puzzle," I said.

"No need to bend your brain too much, Doc. It's dead simple," the tycoon assured me. "People at large are rather oblivious to what's going on around them. They listen to the noise but they can't hear the music."

"Johnny's been playing me a song or two," I nodded. "He's been changing how I look even at little things like the Big Mac."

"Ah, purchasing power," the Mumbai magnate interjected. "Do you mean the *Economist* index?"

I must have looked bewildered, as Johnny quickly jumped in to my rescue.

"More in general," he answered. "I've been discussing inflation affecting purchasing power with Doc. We haven't really gotten that deep into parity across countries yet."

"It's a fascinating example," the Indian woman smiled. "McDonald's entering India has been linked to tripling the number of times Indians eat out. And with a vegetarian running a beef burger company in a country where the majority don't eat beef!"

"Wait," I said. "A vegetarian runs McDonald's?"

The others all laughed.

"Their master franchisee for India, I meant," the magnate smiled. "Fascinating, as I said, but I haven't the time now to discuss it all. You simply *must* read up on it."

"I will," I assured her.

"India has made amazing strides," offered the tycoon. "In the nineties, I remember being mobbed by beggars in the streets of Mumbai, while now they're all selling things instead. Indians want the same things we're used to in the West."

"Quite true," the magnate nodded. "But our country is building for a future many Americans don't even imagine yet."

"Too true," nodded the tycoon.

"Now, I know what the good doctor's background is, but Johnny, what is your field?"

"I started investing as an electrician."

"Ah!" the magnate exclaimed. "You're my nemesis! Here I am, trying to connect countries wirelessly and a man dedicated to wires sneaks into my midst."

"Don't worry about that," Johnny laughed. "We still have plenty of common ground if you're using electricity."

"Fair enough, young man. We'll have to discuss that sometime."

"Follow me, guys," Johnny said, as a crowd slowly began to build up around the perimeter of our conversation.

"Actually, I'll leave you gentlemen to talk without me. There are still some people I must see," offered the woman from Mumbai, nodding her head at each of us in turn, ending with the green-metal maven. "Very good to meet you, Johnny, Doctor Anderson. I'm certain our paths will cross again. But you call me soon, you green-metal maven. We have much to discuss."

She made her way through the circle of eavesdroppers around us, and Johnny led us the other way.

We walked out of the hotel, crossed the street, and ducked into an alley to find a trendy little coffee shop. Johnny recounted how he'd first met the maven at a conference in Munich, Germany, and the life-changing experience he had after hearing his first major keynote.

"It was going to be pretty hard to get rid of someone that tenacious," the green-metal maven noted. "After meeting Johnny in Munich, I used to laugh to myself about whether or not this guy actually thought I was reading all the email he was sending me."

"I started off asking you every question I could think of," Johnny explained. "And then I just went ahead and started sending you my blog every month."

"Wait. What blog?" I asked, genuinely surprised.

"Later, Doc," Johnny suggested.

"So, after a couple of years, one of my bankers in Hong Kong forwards me this piece written by none other than Sparky here," said the tycoon, apparently paying me no mind. "I was bored on a flight, so I read it. And it was good, *damn* good. I took note of it and the next time he emailed me, I finally gave him a response."

"Yeah. A two-word answer if I recall—'nice work,'" Johnny smiled.

"What was the blog about?" I asked.

Instead of answering my question, the maven nudged a middle-aged man standing in front of us in the coffee line.

"Excuse me, sir. I have a little bet with my friends. If you can answer this question, I have to buy a round of coffees for everyone in the line."

"Hey, friend, what you got? I'll do my best to get 'er right."

"How much does copper cost?"

"What?"

"Copper, the red metal."

"Like in a copper pipe? I don't have a dang clue. You got

a question I might actually have a chance to answer?"

"Thanks, pal. Sorry to bother you. Coffee's on me."

"Well, thank you very much," the man grinned.

Johnny put his hand over his mouth to stifle laughter.

"See what just happened there, Doc?"

"How do you expect him to answer that?" I asked, gradually being more comfortable with the first billionaire I'd ever met. He came off as sarcastic, so my gut feeling was to go with that tone in our chatter.

"Sparky's blogs were about exactly that. Very few people—and I'm talking even sophisticated folks—have the slightest clue where everything comes from, let alone the real price or value of it. The investment world has been polarized ever since the commodity prices took off in the early 2000s. Some analysts and investors think China is a bubble and when it explodes, commodities will crash to their long-term averages, while others, me included, feel the growth phase around the world has a decade or two to run. Johnny's blog looks at both sides of the argument with the most important part being that the average guy walking down the street has no idea if commodities are fair value or overvalued."

As we sat down to drink our coffees, Johnny, or as we now called him, "Sparky," just leaned back and let the conversation flow. It was clear that he was letting me enjoy the experience, while at the same time getting his annual update from someone he truly admired. It was a great thrill, and I was proud to be associated with Johnny, appreciating how far he had gone out of his way to open up this entirely new world to me.

"All right," I said, "first, I want to let you know that I thought your presentation was brilliant, so let's just get that out of the way. Now, I don't want sound like a crabapple but I have always considered myself to be an environmentalist, and it's no secret that your entire industry gets painted with a similarly caustic brush, even though I can appreciate that there are good mines and bad mines. But how can I reconcile my beliefs with the possibility of investing in a mining operation?"

"Oh, you think you're an enviro-crusader?" he interrupted. "I am the world's biggest proponent of green energy, and, in turn, I'm a *realistic* environmentalist. I imagine a world where, year after year, we support and explore new technologies that make the possibility of burning less fossil fuels more likely. That's the environmentalist part. I'm realistic because if we want to burn less coal, natural gas, and oil, all of which are finite resources, we have no choice but to have reliable access to the building blocks that make these long-term solutions possible for the generations to come. Now here's a question for you—will there be more or less electric automobiles in the coming decades?"

"Well, the problem with electric cars is range and reliability, but yes, I think anyone could agree we'll see more brands adopting electric models and consumers will likely buy more."

"Great, now how are we going to charge these cars?"

"With electricity, of course."

"What kind of electricity? What most people forget is that we still need to fuel these cars with power—electric power— and most of the world's electricity comes from oil, gas, and coal. I vote for less fossil-fuel electricity and more innovation, more green energy, and more people making it possible."

"Okay, so as Sparky would tell us, the greener and cleaner we create energy, the more that is demanded of copper."

"Yes, society needs to have access to copper. It's not just the red metal, it's also the green metal. There is little wonder it oxidizes into a brilliant turquoise green. Perhaps the big man upstairs was giving mankind a clue as to its many magical uses."

"Point taken. But it's going to take a little more convincing before I become an avid promoter of hard-rock mining."

"Let's assume you are the biggest environmentalist in the world. We can both agree that it is very inefficient dictating policy to people in the developing world, correct?"

"We can use awareness and innovation. Nobody wants to breathe polluted air. However, demanding that people in growing parts of the world install deluxe systems to capture carbon has proven to be a very difficult discussion. That much we can agree on."

"So, perhaps a better way is to inform and educate. At a minimum, even hardened greenies need to fly to their meetings, ride a bicycle to get around, take hot showers, and watch engaging programs to stay current. Do they make bamboo airplanes? Can they print books without paper? Or can you read the latest Greenpeace missive on your e-reader without recharging it from time to time? How can they deliver the seeds for your community garden and where is the water coming from to make it grow? Where do you think the building blocks to every single thing you are looking at come from? The earth, that's where."

"Johnny and I have already had this discussion," I replied. "All the stuff from up here, most of which now has an electrical cord sticking out the back of it, comes from the commodities down there."

"Precisely. Glad we agree on that. The second part of it is to acknowledge that we, the West, or the green movement, cannot prevent them, the developing world, from having what you and I take for granted. They are not marching to the same tune that protesters are drumming—they simply want a better, healthier, and more comfortable life for their families."

"There is no army, no government, and no spiritual force that can stop them," I said.

"Hey! That's *my* line!" the billionaire snapped back.

Johnny burst in to give credit for his mantra to the tycoon. You could see how a decade of being a contrarian had rubbed off on him. It was already beginning to shape the way I was talking after much less time.

"The other thing that we cannot control is the urbanization of these people. In the past twenty years, around five hundred million people have been removed from poverty. The five hundred million before them took a staggering hundred years because change took so much longer before. It's estimated that the next five hundred million will begin to participate in some kind of city life in only one decade. Imagine! The progress that has been created needs to double. Again!"

"So if mankind cannot stop this massive migration, isn't it everyone's duty to come up with better long-term solutions that help these new consumers and everyone else?"

"That's true. We can't stop them. So as an investor, you have two choices—to become a victim or to become a contrarian, or as I prefer to say, a participant. You have probably heard the term NIMBY right?" the tycoon asked me pointedly.

"Not in my backyard."

"Now there's even a more extreme version of that phenomenon called "BANANA"—Build-Absolutely-Nothing-Anywhere-Near-Anyone. This is great if you don't need things like bikes, hospitals, or food—things that tend to come in quite handy in New York City, Tokyo, or even Bangladesh. Yet there is a group of people who want zero development and zero progress for everyone else while they already live in a world with all the comforts entitled to them. To paraphrase Einstein, 'it's easier to split an atom than it is to change a predetermined opinion.' A better position, in my own personal opinion of course, is to extract the things the human race cannot live without in the absolutely best way possible."

"So that's what makes you the world's preeminent environmentalist? You want to mine those things that promote a greener world and you want to do it in the cleanest, safest way possible?"

"Absolutely, but let's go one step further—can we also agree that you and I, as environmentally conscious people, will be very ineffective in dictating terms to government and industry in China, India, and the rest of the developing world?"

"Yes, of course. They would be harder to convince, and even some Western governments would be. We can all remember what happened to the Kyoto Protocol."

"Can we also agree that the human race needs *stuff*, and advocating the BANANA brand of progress is unrealistic and quite literally impossible?"

"Again, I can't argue with that line of thinking."

"And can we finally agree that responsible mineral extraction is what my industry's brainpower and bandwidth should be focusing on in order to promote and provide the products that enhance a greener world?"

"You're on a roll now. And if it's done properly, I would assume it should benefit all the stakeholders involved."

"Now that we're in agreement on the basic principle of mining, let's talk about the lifeblood of any economy. The undisputed king of metals, and the metal that must be used when societies and industry want cleaner power or clearer skies."

"Copper."

"Exactly. Copper, the truly green metal—it's just disguised in red."

"So you're also saying that, hypothetically, we could live without oil, or let's say far less oil, coal, and other fossil fuels if we substituted more copper?"

"Sparky, this is going to be Doc Anderson's lucky day."

"How so?" asked Johnny, who had remained silent while the tycoon and I discussed our environmental concerns.

"You're from the Pacific Northwest, so naturally you're a greenie. You guys are the pioneers of the movement," the tycoon continued.

"So why is it my lucky day?" I asked.

"Because you've positively nailed it. Think about the implications of your statement. Can our society, or any other one for that matter, use far less fossil fuels? The answer we all now know is a resounding 'yes.' What makes it possible? By going greener and cleaner. Among other things, copper is the cornerstone of this strategy. Today, tomorrow, and far into the future."

"Okay, but I still don't understand how knowing this makes today my lucky day."

"I have an hour before my first official meeting. Plus, I missed breakfast, so I'm going to grab an early lunch. Due to Sparky's tutelage, you now know where copper was used, is used, and, most importantly, *will* be used in increasing quantities due to, as you put it, everything we buy coming with an electrical cord sticking out the back. So what we're going to do in the next hour is make you an expert on where copper came from, comes from, and for the purpose of your lucky day, where future resources of copper will come from. Let's call it the CliffsNotes™ version of Copper Mining 101."

"I'm going to learn all of this over lunch?"

"I said the CliffsNotes™ version, Doc. And typically, you need to be one very large investor to get this attention."

"Oh, I'm not complaining. If anything, I'm impressed you can boil it down that much for me."

As we left the coffee shop and walked a couple of blocks to a nearby steakhouse, we re-established the foundation of the Copper Mining 101 lesson. Firstly, global electricity consumption has done nothing in the past one hundred years but go up. No copper meant no electricity, period. Secondly, we agreed, as environmentally conscious individuals, that we do need responsible natural-resource development, and it is the industry's responsibility to provide reliable access to resources so the world can adopt greener solutions.

When we took our seats for lunch, the tycoon requested that both Johnny and I sit across from him. It still seemed odd to me that someone as in-demand as he was would take the time to sit down with us. Johnny was right all along; this was a unique industry. Ordinarily it would have been impossible to gain an even remotely similar level of access to a high-tech billionaire.

As the tycoon knew the restaurant's specialties, we let him order for the three of us.

"You two will love these steaks," he assured us. "Makes me kind of glad Noorita couldn't join us."

"Don't get me wrong when I ask this, because I am humbled you would take the time to explain your philosophy to me, but why exactly are you having lunch with a lowly middle-aged family doctor?"

"Oh. That part, I guess Sparky didn't tell you. You only have one minor responsibility once you have finished your Copper Mining 101 course."

"Here we go. Let me guess, I have to buy your stock?"

"Ha! No, you're not going to move the needle for me if you do that, but you do need to become a proactive environmentalist and that means you have to promise to be an ambassador of the green metal."

"I'm already sold on that. I just hope I can keep up with what you put down!"

As if on cue, our steaks arrived with much fanfare. As we dug in, the green-metal maven continued my education.

"The most important principle for your copper mining

education is to know the difference between supply and demand. Demand, as you already know, is anything that has copper in it while supply means mining new material and recycling old products. Demand for copper has grown by over three percent per year since 1900 and during some periods as high as five. I would suggest that this three percent growth is a very reliable statistic. Let's call it a constant."

"And if we apply the rule of 72," I ventured, "we then know that global demand for copper has doubled approximately every twenty-four years or so."

"Very good. This will be easy for you, but demand isn't the issue. The question is whether or not supply can keep up."

"Come again?"

"Too much copper being supplied against reliable demand should equal low prices while too little copper being supplied should create a premium."

"I thought you said Mining 101. Seems to me you just described Economics 101—the laws of supply and demand."

"I like to use the analogy of musical chairs to explain that. Supply and demand, I mean. If there are 99 people trying to sit in a hundred chairs, could there ever be a premium for chairs? Obviously not. But what happens if all of sudden there are a 101 or a 102 people trying to sit in those hundred chairs? *Voilà*—a premium! Who knows what someone will pay to have a chair when that happens? Over the past forty years, copper has been supplied mainly from old legacy mines and has almost always exceeded demand. All the while demand, as we recall, has been very reliable, growing between three and five percent. So to be crystal clear, for most of the past forty years, there has almost always been just a bit too much or, at times, far too much copper supply available."

"Which makes a premium next to impossible."

"You're acing the test. So let's define what supply really

means in this instance. Copper ore, classified as a rock that has a mineral resource in it, is mined, usually blasted with explosives in a large open pit or underground, and then transported to be processed. Processing takes place one of two ways—the conventional way called flotation or a more modern way called solvent extraction. I'll explain both really quickly. Flotation was developed in the early days of modern mining and has been the most widely used method since. In the late 1960s, a new type of processing was developed called solvent extraction and electrowinning, often called SXEW."

"This is getting pretty deep. You're starting to lose me with all the terminology."

"Relax. This sets up the reason copper prices were low for forty years. The basic difference between the two types of processing is that flotation concentrates copper ore so that it can be economically shipped for final smelting and refinement. Copper ore in the ground, on a global average scale, is now less than one percent copper and over ninety-nine percent waste rock. That means it needs to be bumped up, or concentrated, to have twenty-five to forty percent copper content. Then this super high-grade material is sent for smelting, a term you have likely heard before?"

"That's where they melt the metal down to become pure copper, right?"

"Exactly. Smelting takes this concentrated material to ninety-nine percent, at which point it is refined to pure copper form—which is the red metal that you see in copper cable or piping."

"Okay, so what about SXEW? What's the difference?"

"Solvent extraction is a two-stage hydrometallurgical process that was developed, optimized, and put into large-scale use in the United States during the eighties and Chile during the nineties. This was important as it was able to monetize very low-grade copper ore, often found in waste dumps at major mines, which were previously uneconomical. This process occurs entirely at the mine site as the SX portion extracts leachable copper and then is processed by electrowinning—the EW part—into ninety-nine percent copper metal. When this copper leaves the mine site, it's ready for final refinement to pure copper so there's no smelting needed."

"You weren't joking when you said this would be Copper 101. So how does this affect supply and demand?"

"You already know that copper is sold in pounds. However, on the large international metals exchanges, where excess copper supply goes, it is sold in tonnes—that's metric tonnes, approximately 2,200 pounds. Imagine that for forty years, from the sixties to the early 2000s, copper prices fluctuated in dimes, ranging from sixty cents per pound to just over a dollar."

"Is that why many analysts and pundits feel copper prices should correct to the levels of a reliable forty-year price cycle?"

Johnny smiled at that. He knew I'd been doing my homework.

"Remember the musical chair analogy?" the tycoon asked. "For those forty years, there was almost always a little too much metal supply. There were a few reasons for that. First of all, the big mining companies were run by men who measured their egos by building bigger and bigger mines. The biggest mines in the world today were not built in the recent cycle. Another major reason was the number of end-use customers declined. After World War II, the West became developed to the point that the per-person consumption of copper and other metals stagnated just as all this 'new' supply kept coming on stream. Then, through the eighties and nineties, new technologies like SXEW exacerbated the oversupply. Finally, just when the world was absolutely awash in copper, the Cold War ended and another wave of 'cheap' throwaway metal hit the market. When the Berlin Wall fell on November 9, 1989, the Iron Curtain opened further copper supplies from three of the largest mining complexes in the world. They stopped feeding the military machine and dumped all that metal into an already oversupplied market."

"So for all those years, we had too many chairs and not enough people to sit in them?" I asked.

"The price of copper in 2002 hit an absolute all-time inflation-adjusted low of less than seventy cents a pound, lower than it was for the most of the seventies and eighties."

"So what changed?"

"The industry finally stopped building new copper mines. They didn't stop there, though. Through the nineties, most of the big mining companies curtailed spending and laid off their exploration teams, who are like the research and development divisions of natural resource companies. Where was future supply going to come from? If nobody is constructing new supply, what happens in the future? We remember that even in the lean years, demand always grew. New customers finally did enter the market and they were growing their economies by ten percent a year. Unlike developed countries, these folks were starting from a very low base so they needed the basic building blocks of nationhood. They needed the copper, steel, and oil to grow, in the same way as the United States and Europe at the turn of the last century."

"Let me digest this. The price of copper in 2002 was seventy cents a pound, the same as it was for a large part of the seventies and eighties. How much profit was there for the copper mining industry?"

"Profit? In 2002? You must be joking. A stockbroker friend of mine had a great line about how mining companies could make up their losses by increasing volume! Mining was the laughingstock of the investment world, a perfect page-sixteen story. Years of continued growth in emerging markets slowly but surely absorbed the idiotic oversupply of copper, a three-decade-long hangover. In October 2003, the tipping point occurred. See, the market forgot that supply could be disrupted by numerous unforeseen circumstances like power outages, strikes, or weather."

"So, you're saying that the demand is reliable and you have the statistics to prove it, but supply turns off in a second when something happens."

"Does it ever. The most serious type of supply disruption is an act of God, and boy, did the copper mining industry get one in October of 2003. That acted as the tipping point that ended decades of really low prices. Grasberg, the world's second-largest copper mine in Indonesia, was shut down instantly after a massive pit wall collapse."

"Pit wall collapse?"

"Yes. Due to way too much rain, the entire side wall of that humongous open pit collapsed and the mine was shut down for a period of time. The fallout was that everyone who followed, produced, or purchased copper scrambled to cover the massive copper supply deficit that would surely follow. This one copper mine supplied five percent of the world's copper at the time."

"So that caused the musical chairs to become a premium and the price of copper finally jumped from those absurd lows?"

"You bet! That tipping point drove the price of copper from seventy cents a pound to four dollars a pound in early 2006, an unprecedented jump. Remember, the price of copper used to fluctuate in dimes and then suddenly, it jumped over three dollars a pound in two and a half years."

"What a business!"

"The problem was that nobody in the industry could

believe it either. Most of the executives, professionals, and participants in the copper mining industry thought it was unsustainable. Many of them cashed in their stock options as the price of copper inched its way up, never dreaming it could ever sustain itself past a dollar a pound."

"These companies making copper must have started to make profits hand-over-fist if they were used to selling it for seventy or eighty cents and could now sell for three dollars a pound or more?"

"Some companies prospered, but some well-known copper miners hedged their futures down the toilet. In their wisdom, the same 'insiders' who cashed in their stock options when copper climbed over a dollar were hedging future production at that idiotic eighty-five cents level and even further as prices reached $1.25. There's a great maxim coined by Chicago-based economic historian Donald Coxe: 'Your greatest investment opportunities come from industries where those who know them best, love them least, because they've been disappointed most.'"

"So they locked in the sale of their future supply at eighty-five cents and $1.25 while prices climbed to over $3.00 a pound? What happened to those companies?"

"Take a guess. All of their choice assets were gobbled up on the cheap by competitors. They knew the copper mining industry as well as anyone else, but they had been punished for decades by low copper prices, so they had no confidence. If only they better understood they had hundreds of millions of new customers."

"The new spending class became the new customers of Big Copper."

"The famous investor Sir John Templeton would cringe if he heard someone challenge his idea that 'it's different this time' are the four most dangerous words in investing, but this time it was different. Those hundreds of millions of people were urbanizing, and the copper mining executives failed to see that."

"So, is this still confusing the market? If those executives, who were supposed to be the experts in copper mining, could miss such an obvious change taking place in the world, could the same thing be happening now?"

"I've already told you that the so-called experts who follow copper mining and commodities in general have never been so polarized," the green-metal maven continued. "Seeing is believing, and it will take you a lot more research to become truly familiar with the field. But the one thing that we do know with a high degree of confidence is that a billion new consumers will demand access to basic progress in the next ten to twenty years.

"The answer comes in the reliable concept that these people will continue to consume more things—which I think is unstoppable."

"But to get back on topic, where does all this copper come from? Which countries and how many mines are we talking about?"

He didn't answer that question for a few moments while we pondered it, so he could take a bite of his steak. I wanted to hear the answers, but I wasn't going to begrudge him the food—it was fantastic, after all. I cut myself a piece of my steak, and just as I started to eat, he began again.

"The days when big mining companies could choose where to invest are over. Anyone who thought or still thinks that politics are not relevant to commodity prices or where and how one engages in extractive industries is either a fool or a damn fool. The biggest producer of copper is Chile and the biggest consumer of copper is China—those are the facts. Primary copper production comes from mining, thus the word 'primary,' and secondary production comes from recycling, which is around fifteen percent of the market."

"You're telling us that the existing mines, these so-called legacy mines, are located in established places? So how many mines are we talking about?"

"I'm getting to that in two seconds. We already know that demand has grown by over three percent a year for over a century. The problem we now face is keeping supply up with the pace of demand. In 2012, the world used twenty million tonnes of copper for the first time. If demand growth is three percent, that would suggest we need *six hundred thousand tonnes* of new copper production to keep up with reliable demand, not even factoring in mine closures and reserve depletion. You don't think these mines last forever, do you?"

"So how much *is* six hundred thousand tonnes? Is that a small, medium, or large copper mine? And how many mines are we talking about to produce, say, half of the world's new copper each year?"

"The top fifteen major mines account for about half of primary copper production, which is incredible if you stop and think about it. Only fifteen mines! The largest mine in the world, located in Chile, produced a million tonnes that same year. The bulk of the large mines in the top fifteen produce an average of 250 to 300 tonnes of copper metal per year. So to answer your question the long way around, the industry needs to build two or three significant mines each year to keep up with the very reliable three percent growth rate. What about four or five percent growth like most of the past decade? Do you know how much a copper mine that can yield 250 tonnes a year costs to build?"

"No idea. I'm going to guess quite a bit."

"Modern mines of that size, with all the added costs associated with safety and environmental safeguards, cost five billion dollars or more to build. Gone are the days of building infrastructure in a world with cheap twenty-dollar-a-barrel oil. Twenty and thirty years ago, a billion dollars went a long way to completing a major mine. Today, it's not even the down payment."

"Hold on. A minute ago, you told me the days are over where big mining companies can choose where to invest. That means they're running out of 'safe' and 'easy' places to build new mines. You also told me that the research and development arms of most major mining companies were shut down during the decades of low copper prices. Now you're saying we need to build three medium-sized mines each year just to keep up with demand. And it costs three or four times more for each tonne of production? How are they doing this?"

"They aren't. And that is my *raison d'être*. The longer the period of time that no meaningful new production comes on line, the more the coil is sprung for higher long-term copper prices. As well, the deposits of the future have been left to smaller companies that are focused on the R&D part of the business and less so on the development side. Also, they're often fielded by the very geologists and engineers the big companies fired in the eighties and nineties. People like me will sell our high-quality mineral deposits to the major companies when they are ready to invest in development. But they need higher long-term prices—that's their insurance policy. And yours too."

"These are the speculative junior mining stocks that scare the pants off of people like me," I admitted.

"Sadly, you are right. There's so much stupidity that enters otherwise rational thinking that the majority of small investors are often fleeced."

This was a good time for Johnny to jump in with his memorable George Bernard Shaw quote, "It was created by the upper classes and the lower classes to fleece the middle classes."

"Who you follow for investments is your business," the maven continued. "My job here is to provide the foundation to answer the question—where is all this *stuff* going to come from? Here are the hard numbers. We keep talking about the decade between 2002 and 2012 because so much activity took place in natural resources when metal prices skyrocketed. In 2002, 2.2 billion dollars of capital was raised for speculative exploration, R&D if you want to call it that, in natural resource companies. In 2012, the busiest year on record until that date, 29.2 billion was raised. In fact, between 2002 and 2012, 136 billion was raised worldwide on non-bulk commodity exploration. It has been reported that there were 647 significant new mineral discoveries in that time span. However, only 18 of them were considered to be top-tier. Even though there was a tenfold increase in dollars toward R&D, it simply did not yield a proportionate level of results."

"How can that be?" I asked. "How does any industry spend ten times more money and come up with so little for it?"

"One of the reasons is due to so little expertise. Remember, the mining industry as a whole went through a dark age when there was very little research. Who wanted to become a geologist in the nineties? Everyone wanted to be a computer programmer. Entire geological departments were shut down at major universities. Many who did choose to become extractive industry professionals didn't go to work for mining companies but rather went to work with non-governmental organizations that were trying to stop development."

"I can see that. But there must have been a more important reason there were disappointing results in finding future mineral deposits after a tenfold increase in R&D money?"

"The simple truth is that all the low-hanging fruit has been picked."

"You are trying to tell me that mining is now an extremely difficult business, aren't you?"

"The days of building a mine from discovery to production in five years are long gone. On average, it now takes fifteen years from discovery before a company can recover the first pound of copper that comes out of the ground. Also, the grades are much lower than they were in the past. You recall I said it was 1 percent copper and 99 percent waste rock? That was twenty and thirty years ago. Now, the average grade of a copper mine is 0.6 percent copper and 99.4 percent waste rock, which means miners need to move, on average, almost twice as much rock for the same amount of metal yield they realized in the past."

"Wow. When you look at it that it way, it makes a huge difference. That measly 0.4 percent of a difference in falling grade means they have to mine almost twice as much rock! When you're talking about billions of tonnes, it's a lot!"

"Modern deposits are going to be deeper, more remote, and frequently in countries that don't have the same political surety as Arizona or Chile. Not only is it difficult to find new deposits in remote parts of the world, imagine what it does to costs when you explore and develop, with no infrastructure, in less-friendly places? The distant future of copper mining will need to take place in countries like Mongolia, Pakistan, the Congo, and even Afghanistan. For the obvious reasons of safety and feasibility, there is no guarantee that some of those prolific deposits will ever be developed."

"If the industry is that difficult and riddled with so many challenges, then why even bother?"

"Oh, but that's the fantastic opportunity. If the world needs as much copper in the next twenty years as has been consumed in the past hundred years, and that is the proportional scale, then where is it going to come from?"

I shuddered at the thought that I had a far better

un-derstanding than ninety-nine percent of the investing public about this opportunity.

"Perhaps in the high-quality deposits that have already been discovered," he answered his own question. "A company holding unhedged copper reserves in a politically stable part of the world offers tremendous leverage to future copper pricing. And remember, because the copper is in the ground, there is no storage cost. As such, it's being sold at pennies per pound in the ground. To make these reserves financially viable, there must be higher long-term copper prices. That is your insurance policy to higher future prices."

It made sense, but I couldn't help thinking that if mining was a difficult business, that made it both an opportunity, due to the tremendous leverage being offered, and a hazard, owing to the many pitfalls involved. These in turn seemed to be more plentiful than in other sectors and could easily trip up an investor. However, the opportunity was fortified by the trend of reliable growth in population, electricity consumption, and the largest migration of human beings in history. In the opinion of the four-percenter I was having lunch with, the next great copper deposits to be developed have already been found and all investors like myself had to do was locate them and wait.

"So where will the price of copper go?" I asked the maven as we paid our bill. I pulled out my credit card, but he waved his hand and continued.

"I have no idea, but as long as we have an atmosphere where a hundred people are trying to sit in ninety-nine chairs, we should see 'stronger for longer' copper prices. The second part of the question is—will there be more or less uses for copper? The media can discuss this point until they are blue in the face, but I am quite confident that there will be more people next year and in the next decade. I'm also confident that they will want more basic comforts and that they will have the ability to pay for them. It makes it very hard for me to follow anyone who has not really been to Asia and seen with their own eyes what is really going on."

"I've never been. Never really thought much about it until I met Sparky."

"I bet you don't even have a passport, do you?"

Johnny flashed me a sly grin, which I didn't react to, because I knew he'd been right.

"No, I don't. My wife, ex-wife I mean, and I used to go to Mexico, but that was years ago when we just needed to show our driver's licenses."

"Well, you aren't alone. The vast majority of Americans have never even applied for a passport. You now have a broader education than most people as to why commodities are so important to mankind. The single biggest piece of advice I'm going to leave with you trumps everything else we've talked about."

I could hardly wait. This was the moment when he was going to hand me the holy grail. Did he do the same to Johnny all those years ago, enabling him to find financial freedom in his thirties? Was he going to give me the hottest stock tip of the entire conference?

"My advice to you is to go see the world. And start where it's really going to matter to your future. Go to China."

"China?" I sighed.

10

Planes, trains, and rickshaws

After returning home from the conference, I immediately began the process to obtain my first passport. When I thought about it, it was silly—how could a well-off, fifty-eight-year-old American professional have never even applied for a passport? Being in the company of Johnny and other contrarians, I felt more than a little embarrassed. In fact, I was downright angry with myself. What had I been missing all of these years?

All in all, it was a painless process that took only three weeks. I had paid for the expedited service so I could have it in hand and apply for a travel visa in good time. Johnny had some business to do in China and offered that since he was going a little earlier, I could come along and we could go on a cross-country fact-finding road trip. So I jumped at the opportunity and bought a plane ticket.

The visa application part of our trip-planning was surprisingly easy. Numerous businesses offer visa services and promise a turnover in only a few business days. The main driver for these visa centers wasn't Yankees like me going to China, but the droves of mainland Chinese who were coming to North America en masse as tourists. Who would have thought that?

Our plan was to fly into Hong Kong, now a specially administrated zone within the People's Republic of China, and travel by train to our first destination of Guangzhou. This way, we could also see Shenzhen, which lay between Hong Kong and Guangzhou. Later, we would check out the granddaddy of all electrical generation projects, the Three Gorges Dam, then skip through Shanghai on our way to Beijing, finally ending our trip at the Great Wall of China.

A couple of days before the trip, I had a panic attack and wanted to call the whole thing off when I started to contemplate the fourteen-hour flight. I asked myself what in the bloody hell was I doing? Six months ago, I was a divorcé fumbling around in the dark with a bag full of wires, convinced that the remainder of my days would end up being a predictable series of evenings spent falling asleep on the couch. Now, I was closing my medical practice for two weeks and flying off to China to bear witness to "the single largest migration of human beings in the history of the world."

All the time I had spent with Johnny attending the conference, plus my countless hours of reading and research, had made me a believer, but I was not without some skepticism. If I had one takeaway about the economies of emerging markets, it was that there was always the calamitous threat of a massive market correction, or even worse, social upheaval looming over their development boom. Maybe it was just naysayer hoopla used to sell magazines, but I couldn't shake the image of a tumbleweed floating through a massive unoccupied ghost city. If I'd learned one thing about investing, it was to stay away from bubbles—but that ran contrary to the concept of embracing volatility, the philosophical heart of contrarian investing.

I remembered once again to invest in the story on page sixteen that is on its way to page one. The hurdle was that China was all over the cover pages of global media—the real page-sixteen stories were commodities and energy consumption and how these would be affected by China. If I was really going to understand this convergence, I would need to go see it myself, so I decided to throw caution to the wind and pack my bags for a painful fourteen-hour flight in cabin class.

In the meanwhile, I took the maven's advice and looked deeper into some potential ways copper could serve other purposes. A number of current studies demonstrated that replacing surfaces and objects with the red metal did indeed cut the risk of infection. As he put it, stainless steel was like a magnet for bacteria while copper was a repellent. It was only a matter of time before this became a standard throughout hospitals, or at least well-funded hospitals, all over the world. But that was a small slice of the global economy, so I started studying a sector I should have been following all along—green technology and clean energy.

When you dug a little deeper into green energy, it became clear rather quickly that whether it was wind farms, solar panels, or electric vehicles, anything that was going to make this world greener and cleaner always revolved around electricity, and the common bond in every case was copper.

Green energy's relationship to the Chinese market was equally inextricable. In the case of solar power, over the past few years China grew to dominate the solar-cell market simply due to the sheer size of its manufacturing base. The issue of price had always dogged the marketability of these cells, but because China had gained a foothold in the market, and had the scale to produce in bulk with plentiful access to cheap production materials, *voilà,* they had knocked the price down substantially. These lower prices would naturally make the technology far more appealing to consumers than reasons of pure environmental altruism.

Beyond China's ability to outproduce most other countries, what had made these new cells even more affordable? Copper, of course. By using copper instead of silver for the cell's electrical contact lines, Chinese manufacturers had cut production costs by over half in just a few years.

I'd made a few attempts to calculate how much copper would be needed just to feed the demand of green energy and the numbers left my head spinning. Every bit of research I did helped me gain more confidence and nuanced my perspective. I began to understand more about what *stuff* up here needed which *stuff* down there. But I didn't want to limit myself to any one sector or technology. If I was going to invest, I wanted to invest in all of it, including both the supply and the demand, and my Asian adventure was going to help out in spades.

When I got to the airport, Johnny was waiting for me at the Cathay Pacific counter as planned. As usual, he was even more on the dot than me, self-proclaimed Mr. Punctual.

"Hey, Doc, long time no see. Wow, that's a big suitcase. Did you bring all your tools?"

I looked at my suitcase, admittedly bulky, and compared it to the slick leather duffel bag Johnny had hanging from his shoulder. I threw my hands up in surrender.

"Johnny, we're going for ten days, aren't we? I thought I'd at least bring a suit and a change of shoes."

"That's all right, we have time to adjust that. Now you're going to find out why they have luggage shops at the airport."

"And do what with this?" I said as I pointed to my jumbo-sized suitcase.

Johnny seemed to have an answer for everything. In the span of twenty minutes, we had purchased a sturdy yet compact carry-on trolley-type suitcase. To my astonishment, all the important items fitted with room to spare. We then threw the behemoth into a storage locker and worked our way toward security. Clearly, it was going to be easier to navigate the planes, trains, and rickshaws in this manner. I was relieved.

After we boarded and settled into our seats, I took out a list of points I wanted to reflect on during the flight. For all the things I had accomplished over the past months, this trip would be my final exam. I'd graduated from paying peanuts and getting monkeys to spending good money on a few quality newsletters, and as a result, it felt like I'd gained ten or twenty investment IQ points.

Equipped with this heightened awareness, I'd begun to follow a number of different financial soap operas and even identified a couple of my own four-percenters for each of them. The foundation was firmly in place, and the only thing left to do as an investor was to officially make the switch from passive to active by moving some of my investment dollars into the speculative arena.

Luckily, I was able to catch some solid REM sleep on the plane, so as we touched down on the tarmac a full day after we left Sea-Tac, I was feeling somewhat refreshed. But maybe that was just the adrenaline of adventure entering my bloodstream.

Walking into the airport, I didn't know exactly what to expect. For whatever reason, call it ignorance, I thought it was going to be a dump. What I found was the newest and cleanest airport I'd ever set foot in. As we cleared customs at Hong Kong International, no visa required, Johnny described the sky-high real estate values in the area. And I thought Manhattan was expensive!

After a quick transfer in downtown Hong Kong, we boarded a commuter train for Shenzhen, where we would transfer to Guangzhou. On the way, Johnny gave me a brief history lesson on the region.

"Shenzhen is where it all started. It was China's first Special Economic Zone, which gave it special economic policies and flexible government measures. In 1979, it was just a village and it is now one of the fastest-growing cities in the world. Guangzhou on the other hand, formerly Canton, was the starting point of the Maritime Silk Road and was for centuries China's most important seaport. It's another city where China began its experiment with capitalism back in the eighties. This city used to be the center of the economic universe, and it's on its way to reclaiming that title."

"So when China had the largest GDP in the world for a couple thousand years, this place was pretty important, wasn't it?"

"Sure was, and it is again. It's magnificent what has been built between Hong Kong and Guangzhou in the past three decades alone."

"So how far is our hotel from here, Johnny?"

"We'll be there in less than two hours and we're staying downtown. But when we get to the main station, we're going to take a cab because there's something on the way I want to see."

"Hey, I thought this was a fact-finding mission and not some tourist trip."

"It's going to be a bit of both. But rest assured, we're not going to be spending too much time milling around old temples. If we're going to be touring anything, it'll be the temples of the future."

A string of shiny new taxis was waiting outside Guangzhou's main train station, and to my surprise, most of them were some kind of weird Volkswagen hybrid.

"What, no rickshaws?" I quipped.

"Doc, you'd have a way better chance finding a rickshaw back home than you would in most cities in modern China. This city has a GDP of nearly 250 billion dollars. That's more than San Francisco, which happens to be the rickshaw capital of the US."

Johnny opened the door of the first taxi in line and rattled off some rapid-fire Chinese. The driver looked back at us with a surprised expression, but then shrugged and popped the trunk.

"So you speak Mandarin?"

"I can speak taxi Cantonese or Mandarin. You kind of need both in these parts, and it's going to help us get to where we're going."

"And where's that?"

"To a factory."

"And here I thought we were done with surprises. How foolish of me."

Soon after leaving the train station, we found ourselves on a busy ten-lane highway that had loops and overpasses unfurling in every direction. We sidestepped a massive traffic jam and took an off-ramp into an industrial zone where a ceaseless string of gigantic factories whizzed by in the rear view mirror, while mountains of high-rises dipped in and out of sight in the background. From what I could see, the city stretched on forever toward the horizon.

"I really should have checked this before we left, but how big is this city?"

"Greater Guangzhou has a population of around forty million people. That includes its neighboring city of Shenzhen of course, so double the New York/New Jersey metro area."

"Sweet Jesus, that's a lot of people."

"You probably noticed there was no real stop to the urbanization from H.K. all the way here. A hundred miles without a break—it's breathtaking, really."

After ten or so minutes, our cabbie pulled over to the shoulder and he and Johnny exchanged some more Mandarin before the driver gave another shrug.

"Here we are."

"Where is here?"

"Let's get out and I'll show you."

On the right hand side was a very large factory. On the other side of the road was the construction footprint for what looked to be an even bigger one.

"This plant produces nearly half a million cars per year. That's more than America's busiest automobile factory. And you see that construction site over there? That will soon be another plant that will make even more cars on an annual basis. Right now, every car company on the planet is clamoring to come here and build plants like this—Ford, Volkswagen, Fiat, GM, Toyota, everyone—because in almost every case, this is now their largest market. They're all eager to spend billions here because the Chinese appetite to own an automobile is insatiable. Remember that timeline we talked about—how in 1979, there were just sixty privately owned cars in China and now there are over 250 million vehicles? Car ownership in China has exploded. In fact, between 2005 and 2010 it doubled! Now they make over 50,000 cars a day—that's up a thousand percent in the past couple of decades. And still only a small portion of China's 1.3 billion people actually own a car. So, do you think that this trend is going to come to a grinding halt?"

"Well, that depends on if their economy keeps on growing, doesn't it?"

"If the Chinese economy continues apace at seven or eight percent growth, China is expected to be making more cars than North America and Europe combined by the year 2020. And even then, forty percent of the Chinese population will still live in rural areas. In the past three decades, since Deng Xiaoping awoke their capitalist spirit, over three hundred million Chinese have left poverty to come to places like Guangzhou and Shenzhen. The vast majority of those people are just now buying their first cars. The real question is how long will it take the next 100 million or 500 million people? And then, how about the 2.5 billion people in CHINDIA who are going to join this spending class in basic human progress?"

"I'll guess they are going to need a lot more cars."

"What is the implication of that for oil? Food? The comforts of life? You can apply that migration to anything you want, but just make sure you also apply it to the *stuff* needed to make it all work."

"Which, in the case of an automobile, is an average of 50 pounds of copper. For electric cars, it's over 150 pounds."

"Bingo, Doc. Now, let's hit the hotel and then we'll tackle the streets of Guangzhou."

After another half hour of driving through even more massive highway loops and clogged byways, we arrived in a secluded little neighborhood filled with bustling cafés, chic-looking lounges, and otherwise nondescript office complexes. After dropping off our compact luggage at the hotel, I was thankful I didn't have to drag my old widowmaker around. We then hopped down to a nearby restaurant to get some grub and enjoy the atmosphere. Tomorrow, we'd be taking the train from Guangzhou to Hubei province, where we'd go check out the Three Gorges Dam, so some respite was in order.

Right down to the tight jeans and weird haircuts of the diners, the restaurant we were eating at was eerily reminiscent of the bar we went to back home, where Johnny and I had started talking about trends.

"I didn't know they had so many funky folks in China, Johnny. You sure do have a knack for finding these kind of places."

"They've got everything we've got, only way more of it—as you can expect in a city of twenty million."

"I mean, it's just fascinating to witness how similar these young people are to the kids in any American shopping mall. They dress alike, they act alike, I suppose they even read the same fashion blogs. It's quite remarkable, really."

"Wow, Doc! Fashion blogs? I'm surprised you even knew those existed. You really have come a long way. Just think, twenty years ago, none of this was here. But look a little deeper and you'll notice something else going on that sets them apart from their American doppelgangers."

I looked across the room examining each patron from the shoes up. They definitely paid a lot more for their jeans than I did and appeared even more obsessed with their smartphones than their American millennial counterparts.

"O wise one, I give up. Please enlighten me," I said.

Johnny pointed at a group of young ladies sitting at the bar.

"You see those girls?" he asked. "Look at their handbags. Those aren't knock-offs. They're genuine Fendis. Or how about the guy sitting at the table over there? Check out his watch."

"So they're rich kids?"

"Westerners aren't uniquely equipped to generate wealth, Doc. If you took a world tour four or five hundred years ago, you may not have been that impressed with European cities and the American colonies. However, you would surely have been blown away with the Far East as many a European trader was. We were just in the right place at the right time for our industrial revolutions while Asia was taking a nap sorting itself out. China's spending class of four hundred million and growing is experiencing a consumer mania for luxury goods."

"What kind of luxury goods?"

"You name it, they buy it. The Chinese addiction to luxury brands started out with the über-rich in the cosmopolitan neighborhoods of Shanghai and Beijing, but now the trend has gone nationwide. Designer brands are even setting up shop in China's third-tier cities, something you don't see in Milwaukee or Toledo."

"Is there really that much demand?" I asked.

"There's so much interest in designer goods here that they've started opening up shopping malls that exclusively stock luxury brands. Some analysts are predicting that China will eclipse every other major market by a quantum for luxury goods. But right now, it's more about claiming space for the future than profiting today."

"How so?"

"If you build it, they will come. If you want to understand anything about China, you need to memorize that line like a Buddhist mantra. It can be applied to infrastructure, real estate, and even expensive handbags. Brands like Louis Vuitton and Gucci know that China will continue to be their most important growth market. So in the meantime, they'll open stores across the country and rent space in these luxury malls, even if they aren't profitable, just to have a presence."

"That's very interesting, but it also sounds like the boutique version of the ghost cities we always hear about."

"It's all psychology, Doc."

"How so? You mean these guys are getting brainwashed?"

"The fact that so many Western analysts and journalists are still wringing their hands over ghost cities or ghost malls or ghost anything is, to use the language of your profession, a symptom of something entirely unrelated to the medium- and long-term planning of China's *planned* economy."

"It's a communist country and they do have something called five-year plans, Johnny."

"Exactly. Growth could never stay at ten or twelve percent in perpetuity, could it? What is frequently forgotten by the reporters and analysts is the base is getting bigger. Remember the overall economy grew by almost ten percent for thirty years—the base is now a monster, second only to the United States, so six or seven percent growth is still a bigger number than the ten percent growth of the economy of ten years ago."

"All right, if we're playing doctor, what's your diagnosis regarding how Westerners see China?"

"The Chinese are speculators and a speculator is inherently optimistic about the future, while we Westerners have become pessimistic after decades of stagnation. Most folks back home simply have forgotten what it is like to see your salary double every five or six years. Look back at the America of fifty and a hundred years ago, with the exuberance in building the country with our superprojects, the same thing the Chinese are doing now."

"You already told me that when America invested four percent or more of GDP into infrastructure, the American economy grew by roughly the same rate, same as the Chinese economy has mirrored the eight or nine percent of GDP they've been investing into building. You're saying this is a matter of perception?"

"Definitely. Perception is the fundamental difference between East and West, and it's the fundamental difference between being passive and being a participant. As J.M. Keynes said, 'Investing is an activity of forecasting the yield over the life of the asset; speculation is the activity of forecasting the psychology of the market.'"

"So if we go to one of these luxury shopping malls, and there are no customers, that's still a good thing? Those companies are speculating that the market will get stronger in the future?"

"In my opinion, these projects are just a form of infrastructure—the infrastructure of consumerism. Another problem with the West's perception of the Chinese economic miracle is that we think it of it as a one-off event, rather than an ongoing process. A generation ago, nobody here was even thinking of buying their first car, let alone splurging on designer clothes or expensive wine, another mania in China. Now, millions have bought their first car, and we're sitting in a lounge filled with youth wearing designer brands. Yet it's still just a drop in the bucket of what will happen as another five hundred million people join the spending class and gradually become bona fide consumers. The ongoing migration from rural to urban continues to be just the first step. Now China is working on building the world's next great consumer society."

We chowed down some dumplings and had a few bottles of Tsingtao while I mulled this over. After paying the bill, we hit the street and walked by a string of vendors haggling with would-be patrons. Then we passed a string of storefronts bustling with shoppers and young people who were spilling out of one bar to cross the street to the next. I became aware of the "ex-pats," citizens of other countries now residing here. Quite a few crossed our path, a high percentage of whom were African, something else I didn't expect.

"I didn't expect it to be so diverse," I said as we cruised back towards the hotel.

"There are probably sixty thousand ex-pats here, half of which are African."

"Why is that?"

"It's the Chinese dream, Doc. We always hear about how hungry China is for African resources. Well, Africa is equally hungry for Chinese goods and manufacturing techniques. Since the nineties, the keenest traders in countries like Nigeria realized they could cut out the middleman and come straight to where the *stuff* they need is made to get it at the best price possible."

• • •

In just over a week, we were going to travel cross-country from Guangzhou to Beijing, so our itinerary demanded an early rise, which meant lots of coffee. I wanted to see if I could find a typical local café in the neighborhood before we left but was only able to find a Starbucks. To think that when they first started to spread in Seattle, I thought it was an idiotic trend that would never last. That's one of the stocks that got away.

Next on our list was the Three Gorges Dam, and to get there from Guangzhou, we needed to take a series of trains. I had ridden Amtrak a number of times in the past, but it had been at least ten years since I had last been subjected to rail travel. My experience with Amtrak had always been challenging, to put it nicely—cross-country trains were late, stalled, cramped, and very slow. The sight of the train station gave me flashbacks to one very bitter Christmas Eve spent stranded in Boston due to a malfunctioning snowplow.

Still, after arriving at the Guangzhou station the day before, I'd come to expect that every form of transport we would come across in China would be brand spanking new, and the bullet train we took on the first stretch of the trip did not disappoint. Not only was the train itself a gleaming space-age marvel, but the entire rail network seemed like it had been built the week before I arrived. In the course of five years, China's high-speed network had grown bigger than all of Europe's, now stretching more than ten thousand kilometers (about six thousand miles) linking numerous cities. China uses the metric system, just like Europe and most of the world. I thought about that cold night in Boston and was supremely envious of the Chinese—a sensation I never would have predicted I'd ever have to suffer through. When one travels by train from Boston to New York, it's like setting your watch back seventy-five years as the click-clack of our slow and antiquated railroad system echoes the need for a complete reset button to be pressed on so much of our ailing rolling stock.

In just five hours, we traveled nine hundred kilometers (about 550 miles), passing through Shaoguan, Zhuzhou, Changsha, Xianning, and many more cities I wouldn't dare try to pronounce. A modern cross-country train ride in most other parts of world must be similar to what I experienced. The food, however, which was served from the usual rolling cart, was not at all typical. The offerings ranged from chicken beaks and gizzards to pig's feet. My personal favorite from this exotic, yet intimidating, selection was pig's ears. All these delicacies were neatly vacuum-packed with little clear windows letting you know what you were about to enjoy. Check, please!

I knew about Shanghai and Beijing, and now Guangzhou, but had never heard of any of these other cities, and all of them had millions of inhabitants. It was simply amazing. It made sense to travel by train as it allowed us to observe China's landscape. If we had flown between our destinations, easily doable with all the modern airports built in past years, we never would have experienced the vast changes in landscape and culture. These cities were only going to get bigger and the building blocks were already in place to make it happen.

We arrived at Wuhan's main train station, one of three in the city, only to discover that it would take a bit longer to get to the dam than expected, so we decided to go off-schedule and spend the night. It was another city that I, and likely most people back home, had ever heard of. Wuhan, a city of over ten million people, was like the Chicago of

China because of the amount of expressways and rail lines that passed through it. Like Guangzhou, they also made a lot of cars there, and all the big names like Nissan, Hyundai, GM, Volkswagen, etc. had set up shop, culminating in a production capacity that would likely break three million vehicles in the near future, earning the city the nickname "China's Detroit" though it would soon surpass the Motor City's output, even during that city's pinnacle years.

Around the corner from our hotel, we found a little ramshackle restaurant set up in an alley and grabbed a couple of stools. I say restaurant, but it was more of a laissez-faire food court where you could buy dishes from a variety of vendors. Fried frog on a stick was on the menu, but I wasn't quite ready to test my stomach's mettle against such exotic street meat. One of the customers spoke some English and let us know that the city's specialty was hot and dry noodles, so we ordered two bowls. It turned out he was a taxi driver and was very eager to tell us about how congested traffic in the city had become over the last few years due to all the new cars and construction.

Our speaking English and obviously being foreigners seemed to attract a small crowd. There was a real desire on the part of anyone learning English to practice their newly learned skills on some native speakers. Even though they were speaking in broken sentences with a limited vocabulary, we were able to talk to them about their ambitions and goals. Some of them wanted to study in America while others were starting and growing their own businesses right there in Wuhan. What they all had in common was a positive outlook on the future; the feeling they would be wealthier and happier than their parents. And all of them wanted that to happen in China. I remembered that there were 415 million millennials in China, and over 100 million of them already had college degrees.

One neatly dressed woman in her late twenties wanted to have a family, a boy and a girl, something not possible for the generation before her under China's notorious one-child policy. Due to falling birth rates and increasing resistance, the policy had been amended to enable families to have more children. I thought to myself, what is the implication of this policy when factored over a fifty-year time frame?

A couple of train transfers and a four-hour bus trip later, we arrived at the Three Gorges Dam "scenic area," which consisted of a few viewing platforms and a garden. The place was teeming with tourists, mostly Chinese with the odd Westerner mixed in. Beyond the visitors snapping photos was the colossal dam, the largest concrete and steel structure in the world. Built over seventeen years by forty thousand workers, it was the most ambitious civil engineering feat I'd ever heard of. I was now staring at it in amazement.

"What do you think, Doc?"

"It's massive."

"One hundred years in the making, quite an accomplishment."

I'd read up on the facts about the project before we left the US, and they were astonishing—it cost $37 billion to build, and required the relocation of over a million people. The Three Gorges Dam has the world's largest instantaneous generating capacity of 22,500 megawatts, ten times the size of the Hoover Dam, and three times bigger than the Grand Coulee Dam in Washington state, America's largest. It has the capacity to power four cities the size of Los Angeles. It consisted of 27 million cubic meters of concrete and enough steel to build sixty-three Eiffel Towers. I'd read that beforehand, but seeing it with my own eyes was very different from reading a fact sheet. The scale was magnificent and the implications even more so.

"This is true baseload green energy, meaning it runs at

full capacity twenty-four hours a day, seven days a week," Johnny said. "The commonly used alternative, coal generation, would require thirty-one million tonnes of coal to be burned each year to produce the same amount of electricity—meaning this dam is saving the world one hundred million tonnes of greenhouse gas emissions," Johnny said.

"I remember going to Hoover Dam when I was a kid with my parents," I replied. "There was something so optimistic about it, like it was a giant symbol of American exceptionalism."

"We don't make infrastructure investments like this anymore. There's too much partisan politics and far too much debt, not just back home but all over the developed world. Plus it sure does help when you have a country of engineers to successfully imagine and execute a project of this scope. We have countless bridges in desperate need of repair, our ports need expanding, our airports need modernizing. Hell, many states and counties can barely fix their potholes. We've totally forgotten how critical infrastructure is to a growing economy. Meanwhile, China continues to spend eight percent of its GDP on projects like this."

"We used to have the capital and the know-how, now they have the capital and they already know how!" I joked.

"Newspapers love to predict the impending collapse of China's economy, but meanwhile the Chinese march forward, easily able to finance these big state projects."

"So how are you so confident that progress will continue?" I asked.

"Look what happened to America's economy after the Hoover dam was built. It was followed by an era of unparalleled progress and growth. If you build it, they will come. If you build the world's largest hydroelectric dam, there is a reason—it's because you know consumption of electricity since the invention of the lightbulb has done nothing but increase. What are the better choices for the reliable baseload power needed to feed over one billion people?"

Solar power and wind power, great as complementary power sources, simply do not have the scale for 24/7 reliability. The alternatives—coal, oil, and natural gas, that last to be facilitated by the Russian–Chinese natural gas pipeline being built—all come with the negative side effects of carbon emissions. The other zero-emission source, nuclear, has its own controversial pros and cons. What was clear is that the 2.5 billion people of CHINDIA would need enormous amounts of electricity and it seemed like a better solution for it to come in the form of the Three Gorges Dam rather than through polluting fossil fuels.

The final thought we were left with during our Three Gorges field visit was the added benefit of flood control. The guide mentioned that over the decades, hundreds of thousands of lives had been lost and tens of millions left homeless due to the unpredictable nature of the mighty Yangtze River, the longest in Asia.

• • •

In the morning, we got back on the bullet train and were in Shanghai, the most European city in China, by early afternoon. I was still blown away by the size and speed of the rail system, imagining what it would be like if I could hop on a train in Los Angeles and be in San Francisco within a few hours.

In contrast to Guangzhou and Wuhan, Shanghai seemed less like an industrial town and was more flamboyantly prosperous. Walking down the streets, you could sense that this was a real seat of economic power. It was glossy, shiny, and felt successful. I couldn't help but notice how many art galleries and symbols of global culture there were as we worked our way through a series of vibrant neighborhoods toward Pudong, an area full of new skyscrapers.

We walked the length of the Bund, the area of Shanghai fashioned after turn-of-the-twentieth-century Europe. This famous riverside promenade echoed the classic buildings of Paris and Vienna, juxtaposed against the glass giants across the river in newly constructed Pudong.

Later that evening, Sparky took me through a very hip neighbourhood, Xintiandi, where a smorgasbord of ex-pats, locals, and tourists wined, dined, and shopped themselves into oblivion. At my request, Sparky lead me to what one of the top fashion blogs had called the best wine and spirits bar in China—a stunning venue nestled in a beautiful building with a gleaming star-studded constellation logo beckoning revelers. Inside, I witnessed a similar scene to that in Guangzhou—young, affluent youth clad in the latest fashions, texting away like mad on their smartphones, all while quaffing single-malt scotch and fine wines, both the top French and Italian labels and more familiar wines from the US. This was a veritable shrine for the city's young, newfound wealth.

Shanghai's population is twenty-four million, making it the largest city by population in the world. Even when you think of the supercities like Tokyo, Moscow, Mexico City, and New York, it's hard to imagine a place with more possibility than Shanghai. It's little wonder so many Chinese-born US university graduates come back to stake their claim on the future right here.

One day and night in Shanghai was far too short to appreciate all she had to offer but the show needed to get back on the road, the *railroad* that is. As I quickly learned, the most prestigious rail link between any two cities in the world surely had to be the supertrain between Shanghai and Beijing.

"My first trip over here," Johnny explained, "we took the 'old' train that *only* did two hundred kilometers (about 120 miles) an hour. It took twelve hours door to door. For our trip today, we'll be riding on the fastest scheduled train in the world. We'll average three hundred kilometers (about 190 miles) per hour and we'll be door to door, thirteen hundred kilometers (about eight hundred miles) away, in only five hours."

"Five hours at three hundred kilometers an hour?" I quickly did the calculations in my head. "That would be like traveling from Washington, DC to Miami in the same time, or Boston to New York in about seventy-five minutes!"

We scheduled the morning train so the whole trip would be in daylight. Like the previous train rides, there was endless progress on both sides of the tracks. We passed these massive blocks of apartment housing thirty or forty units wide and dozens of buildings thick. Perhaps they were some of the ghost cities I had heard so much about. In Beijing, I wanted to find out.

Taking that morning train enabled us to arrive just after lunch and enjoy an early afternoon walk. I began to understand what the maven had meant when he talked about the Airpocalypse—the thick steely-gray smog made it difficult to see skyscrapers in the distance. While smog had been prevalent in other areas we visited, it was noticeably worse here in Beijing. Everywhere, people were wearing face masks, which had me self-consciously worry about my lungs.

We walked through a minefield of leisurely shoppers, stalls, and stands selling everything from tourist kitsch to bizarre electronic innovations like a cellphone that doubled as a cigarette holder. Johnny taught me my first bit of Mandarin. *Bu yao* meaning *don't want* which, when used repeatedly, was effective at keeping the hawkers at bay. They weren't my primary concern, anyway.

"Should I have brought a surgical mask? Or an oxygen

tank? The locals seem to be protecting their lungs from all this smog."

"Nah. You'll be fine, Doc. Just don't breathe too deeply."

"Well, *that's* reassuring."

"You should love this. It's a dream come true for a greenie like you!"

"How on God's green earth is walking through toxic smog fumes a dream?"

"Because it's conditions like these that are going to make China kickstart the whole green economy into warp speed. This level of pollution is already uninhabitable and if they don't do something about it, there will be more than just health issues to deal with. Like they say, 'in every crisis, there's an opportunity.' The Chinese government is already making cleaner air a priority and green tech innovation will be a pillar of their future economy, which means better, cheaper green tech for the entire world."

"So what's happening with solar power, for instance, is going to happen to other green tech ideas?"

"You betcha. What they did for hydroelectricity in the south, they'll do for wind power in the north. China's installed capacity of wind power will more than double as they make the single biggest push in renewable energy in the coming years. That means they will have more investment in renewables than the United States and the European Union combined."

"That's a lot of windmills," I said.

"And with a lot of windmills comes . . ."

"A lot of copper," I interrupted.

"Each windmill is its own self-contained power plant that has to be multiplied over and over, unlike giant projects where backbone items are not replaced over and over. Protection against lightning strikes, power distribution, and so on means more copper per kilowatt generated by each of these factors. Whenever you see a wind turbine, whisper that to yourself."

The contemporary industrial revolution I had witnessed over the past week was the fastest in history. According to Johnny, in only thirty years, China had gone from backwater to superpower, from little overall economic footprint to being the largest consumer of almost every major commodity.

Yet, people are skeptical about the sustainability. On Henry Kissinger's 1971 visit to China, he asked Zhou Enlai, Mao's foreign minister at the time, his assessment of the French Revolution. Zhou replied, "It's too early to say." The Chinese have always taken long and calculated steps, so the full consequences of the thirty-year industrial revolution to date are also "too early to say."

After strolling past some of the more touristy spots of the city center, we took a bus to Badaling, a nearby section of the Great Wall of China. Visually, it was even more astonishing than the Three Gorges Dam, but for an entirely different reason. As far as I could see, there was an uninterrupted stream of people cascading through the wall's concourse. It was a sight to behold and a picture in a book could never capture this moment.

"My God," I said. "This place is packed like a college football game."

"Chinese tourists," Johnny nodded. "The world's most profitable renewable resource. Anyone feeling bearish about the Chinese economy should really just look at how much they're spending on their holidays."

"I'm guessing it's a lot?"

"One in ten global tourists is now Chinese. There are now almost a hundred million outward-bound trips, half of which are for holidays or leisure. Which means Chinese tourists now spend more money worldwide than Americans. But here's the important part—eighty percent of these tourists say that shopping is the main reason for their trip. And guess how many Chinese have passports?"

"Not many?"

"Just five percent. They spend nearly a 150 billion dollars around the world, and it's only at five percent. That's going to double in the next few years, and when that happens, the world will need to be prepared. Chinese tourism is a huge opportunity for any country wise enough to adopt the policies to encourage it. I hope the US will be one of them."

Americans have enjoyed the freedom to travel since our country was founded but even though I could have traveled all these years, I had been nowhere and seen nothing. All of a sudden going to Las Vegas or Miami Beach seemed far less exotic than what was really out there. My passport was going to get lots of mileage before it expired. This trip was the first of many and I was sure I would be running into lots of camera-carrying people from the Red Dragon.

• • •

On the last day of our trip, Johnny and I separated because he had meetings to attend with a mining firm in which he had invested. So I had Beijing all to myself.

I did a quick tour of the city's architectural marvels, most of which didn't exist ten years ago. The National Stadium, or "Bird's Nest," was the largest steel structure on Earth. While it was impressive for its sheer size, I preferred the Galaxy SOHO complex. Built in 2012 by the renowned architect Zaha Hadid, it was a gigantic aluminum megamall that was home to some 370,000 square feet of commercial space. From a distance, it looked like some futuristic alien spacecraft, something that would be very hard to get approved or financed in most parts of the world.

Walking through its cavernous interior, I couldn't help but be reminded of the Great Wall. It was obvious to anyone that the Chinese had a unique ability to plan on a grand scale and execute the construction of their gargantuan dreams. They have the ability to build right here and right now without consideration for NIMBY, let alone BANANA, issues.

Visually, the two structures couldn't be more different; one was a giant temple of consumerism, awaiting the world's next great consumer society to materialize, and the other was a man-made object so lauded that rumors claim it's visible from space, built to defend from raiding bandits.

However, at their core, they were both grounded in the philosophy of "build first," a philosophy the Chinese had been employing for centuries. It turned out the Great Wall was a great idea—it allowed the Chinese empire to exist and flourish, and I got the feeling that this great mall would end up playing a similar role for the China of tomorrow.

I now considered myself to be a quasi-expert on emerging markets and their new spending-class consumers. While Johnny was going to stay on for a while to conduct some business, I'd be heading home and applying my new knowledge to my life.

On my flight home, it was an especially nice feeling to be bumped up to business class as I boarded the plane for Seattle. Sitting next to me was a tidy-looking fellow in a slim-cut business suit.

"How's it going?" I asked.

"Tired," he somberly replied. "Another long trip for only two days of meetings."

"You were here on business?"

"Yup. I come every two months or so, but always for a

forty-eight-hour power session. How about you?"

"I was here doing research on a financial soap opera."

"You're an actor?"

"No. I just follow financial markets like someone might follow *Days of Our Lives*, or any other daytime soap opera."

"Oh, cool. What kind of markets are you in? I'm an investment banker specializing in clean tech."

"So you know a thing or two about green energy?" I asked, thinking to myself that this fourteen-hour flight was going to fly by.

"I know enough to be dangerous."

"What are your thoughts on commodities as the lynchpin for green energy?"

"Friend, let me tell you, the most important thing for green energy is green money!"

"Really?"

"How do you think they make this stuff? With good old fashioned cash and a brilliant R&D department."

"Well, we're going to have some time between here and Seattle. Let me tell you about the green metal . . ."

Awakenings

Wednesdays were different now. They were still my favorite day of the week, but for an entirely new set of reasons. My daily ritual started with tending the garden I'd planted in my backyard. Once an overgrown patch of crabgrass, it was now overflowing with vegetables and herbs. Today, I was particularly concerned with the progress of my tomato vine, which I had high hopes for.

I no longer wasted my mornings trying to find a parking spot for the Lincoln because the Lincoln was long gone. I'd finally put my money where my mouth was and decided to buy an electric car—a Tesla Model S to be exact. It was as eco-friendly as a vehicle could get and, as a bonus, parking lots throughout the city offer V.I.P. charging stations for visionaries like yours truly—Johnny would have to grease a valet's palm to get the same treatment. Tesla's founder,

Elon Musk, was a card-carrying member, some might even say the flag-bearer, of Johnny's 4% Club. He had finally launched the electric car into mainstream reality. The future truly was now.

I used to wonder what had held back the commercial viability of zero-emission vehicles all those years, not that I bought into any of the conspiracy theories that abounded. Johnny and I used to talk about how in the coming years, every urban vehicle—buses, garbage trucks, postal vans, etc.—would all become electric. Beyond the economics, basic common sense said surely every city dweller would appreciate avoiding smelly exhaust fumes.

We questioned the technical capabilities that weren't getting to the right point for mass adoption and threw out all the phrases like "range anxiety" to try and make sense of it. At some point, I connected the dots. While society sat around waiting for tech to catch up to where we wanted it to be, the tech was waiting for us to adopt it so that it could grow. After hybrid cars hit the market, people jumped on board and they picked up speed. In no time, every carmaker had various models, each with newer tech and greater capabilities. All it took was someone to be at the front of the curve. So why not me?

Generally speaking, technology from computing to communications and across the spectrum to greener and cleaner energy had doubled every eighteen months or so, while costs to the consumer were halving at unimaginable rates. The larger automotive manufacturers could no longer ignore the future of transportation. Henry Ford once said, "If I asked customers what they wanted, they would have said a faster horse."

My new car, an amazing collection of technologies, had put all my recent education into perspective. There are hundreds of high-tech batteries in the Tesla, enabling a gasoline-free range of about 250 miles, more than enough for any use I had in mind. Even so, for long-distance travel there are high-speed charging stations across the nation where an eighty percent charge is possible in about thirty minutes, about the same amount of time a typical stop and gas break takes.

Speaking of renewable energy as a technology, I had also installed a set of solar panels on the top of my garage some time ago. The cost of solar energy, on a per watt basis, had dropped by a factor of ten in the past decade. When coupled with a wall-mounted battery system, I could offset my carbon footprint by charging my car, now the single largest energy draw in my home, or offset my dependence on the power grid. Even living in the predominantly overcast Pacific Northwest, I was now able to entertain the possibility of going completely off-grid. I wasn't there yet, but considering my recent enlightenment, I knew fast-moving technology, almost always powered by an electrical cord, would get me there. Naturally, it all fed back into my investments. You don't even want to know how much copper was used between the car, the batteries, the solar panels, and all the interconnecting cabling to make this clean energy reality possible.

El Grande was still there, but I was nearly at the summit. I was the envy of the neighborhood when there was a power failure and only my lights stayed on, another benefit of my new energy system. Everything electronic was automated and linked to my iPad and iPhone—lights, heating, entertainment system, the entire home was now space-aged. The kitchen was still only half-done, but the remaining work was purely cosmetic so I wasn't losing any sleep over an exposed pipe or two.

When I was done tending to the crops, I would usually settle into my home office, flip open my laptop, and begin to read my newsletters. Two of them would appear in my inbox by the time I'd poured my first cup of coffee. After returning from China, my first order of business had been to find another doctor who was willing to share my practice with me. It was a big decision, but the trip had tipped the scales. I didn't want to be one of those dusty old family doctors working well into his seventies, and if I was going to become a participant, a true-blue contrarian investor, I knew I would need more free time to follow my financial soap operas.

Luckily, I found a young buck named Vijay, fresh from his practicum, and brought him on board. He had a calm and pleasant bedside manner, and, most importantly, he was an ardent Mariners fan. He was able to fit in right off the bat, so I was more than comfortable to leave him in charge for half the week.

It was also convenient that Vijay was raised in Mumbai, which was my next major project as I dissected the potential of the other end of CHINDIA. China had opened my eyes, but our quickly changing world also included India, Thailand, Indonesia, and the whole African continent. I salivated when thinking of the pages of my passport filling up with entry stamps. Vijay would be able to coach me through India, the rest I would try to figure out along the way.

My second order of business after getting back was to stop using my online brokerage account for all of my investments and find a full-service stockbroker who was an expert on the things the new spending class wanted to buy. On Johnny's advice, I took a trip to Vancouver and met with a close friend of his who had proven connections and a solid reputation. Everyone called him "the Birdman," for reasons I still don't understand, but it was likely due to his owl-like wisdom.

The first thing we did after discussing my investment goals was to restructure only a portion of my portfolio for "higher risk" opportunities. I still had Microsoft and Coca-Cola, but instead of chasing eight percent with all of my investment dollars, I switched to a regimen wherein I'd put small percentages of my available funds into stocks related to my main financial soap operas—the ascent of man, of course, and the one I was most keen on, the greening of our planet, with copper playing a starring role.

Over and above some really good ideas and quick execution, an added advantage I had in using the Birdman's connections had been his access to private placements and exclusive initial public offerings and new stock issuances. The benefit of investing this way was the warrant to purchase additional shares in the future, which meant that I, the investor, had the right, but not the obligation, to buy additional shares—two, three, or even five years into the future, and near the entry-price level. This was the ultimate call on the future and my online account could never offer me that. Plus, I had full access to the best and brightest minds in the research departments, offering everything from bottom-up company analysis to forty-thousand foot macroeconomic views.

As far as choosing my master themes, the trip had taught me one unassailable truth—nothing was going to stop China from eventually becoming the world's largest consumer society. It's simple arithmetic. The peasant who became the factory worker would soon become the shopper, and the same process was going to repeat itself across the globe with the next five hundred million, even one billion people. They all wanted to join in the basic economic progress that had allowed me to live such a great life. All those people wanted and deserved the same things as Americans, and there was no army, no government, and no spiritual force that could hold them back.

Right down to the second, the front door opened and in walked Johnny for the favorite part of my Wednesday routine, our weekly briefing.

"Okay, Doc, you said you had a hot tip for me today so it better be good," he said, pouring himself a cup of coffee.

"I was going to send it to you by email, but then I thought, why don't I just write it down for you?"

"Another research report to dissect?"

"Better still, I've decided to give Brady and Jenna an education they can put to use. What better gift could a father give them? I've come up with 'Doc Copper's ten things every modern investor should know,'"

"You going to write them down? Maybe we should frame them next to the top five that changed my life."

"That's a great idea! I was also going to put them in my office. Number one—if you pay peanuts, you get monkeys. Number two—get a passport. Number three—the greener and cleaner we create energy . . ."

"The more that is demanded of copper. That's *my* line, Doc!"

Afterword

I could not conclude *My Electrician Drives A Porsche?* without commenting on the repeated references to China's insatiable growth. For most of the twentieth century, when the American Republic invested in excess of four percent of GDP on infrastructure, its economy grew in robust fashion and it led the world in almost every economic category. In more recent times, that investment has shrunk to two percent of GDP or less, while expensive wars have been waged and costly crises addressed.

In Asia and other parts of the developing world, investment into the building blocks of their economies has been eight percent, nine percent, or more of GDP, and we have all been witness to the impact of this breathtaking growth. The contemporary argument is that there has been too much development, particularly in China's real estate market. Will a painful hangover need to occur to mop up the excess, leaving an ongoing drag, specifically on future demand for commodities?

Unless people have extensively travelled the world, both east and west, they cannot have a truly balanced perspective of where we currently stand. Suggesting that America's infrastructure is rusting away, saddled by trillions of dollars of debt—owed in most part to China, which continues to reinvest in seemingly unstoppable urbanization—is simply a fair representation of the facts.

But here is the good news. The greatest example of unbiased wealth creation in history has been the American experience and this exceptionalism will yet again enable them to be reinvented. Jokingly, I once asked a mathematical whiz kid what the value of the United States was; that means every road, every bridge, every building—the entire country. A few weeks later, he replied two hundred trillion dollars!

Even the staunchest skeptic cannot deny the magnitude of the economic potential of countless billions of people who still dream of coming to America, urban China, or urban anywhere to make their fortune. If this book can bestow only one lasting ideal for the reader, let it be that the *pursuit* of liberty itself, and all the things it represents, can never rust as long as there is someone somewhere, dreaming about a better tomorrow.

Godspeed . . .

Gianni Kovacevic

Gianni Kovacevic is an investor, author, and sought-after public speaker. He has enlightened audiences around the world with his unique insights into wide-ranging topics such as modern energy, the rise of the new spending class, and how the environment and investment often go hand-in-hand. An avid proponent of realistic environmentalism, Kovacevic is frequently interviewed by the media with his unique way of applying the algebra way of thinking to solving global problems. Fluent in English, German, Italian, and Croatian, Kovacevic makes his home in Vancouver, Canada.

For more information on Kovacevic, go to:
www.kovacevic.com

". . . you know a dream like this seems kind of vaguely ludicrous and completely unattainable. But this moment is directly connected to those childhood imaginings. And for anybody who's on the downside of advantage and relying purely on courage: it's possible."

Russell Crowe at the 73rd Annual Academy Awards